SALMA GUNDI

THE STORY OF A MIXED RACE CHILD GROWING UP IN NEW YORK CITY AND MINNESOTA

BY SANDRA ROGERS-HARE

ROGERSHARE PUBLISHERS * SAN LEANDRO, CALIFORNIA

Authorization to use photo, Ralph Jumps, by Stephen Shames,
Stephen Shames Photographer

Graphic Design by Melissa Davis and Nils van Lingen,
http://www.onderaards.nl

Genghis Khan Urban Guerrilla Research Society
Rogershare Publishers
San Leandro, California

~http://en.wikipedia.org/wiki/Salmagundi definition

SALMAGUNDI

Salmagundi is derived from the French word, *salmigondis*, which means a disparate assembly of things, ideas or people, forming an incoherent whole. Salmagundi is used figuratively in modern English to mean a mixture or assortment of things.

DEDICATION

This memoir is dedicated to my children, Cassidy and Harold, who have always managed to grow towards the sun. To paraphrase the words of Loretta Lynch, the first female African American Attorney General of the United States, I wouldn't trade the love of my children for all the riches of the world because for me, they *are* all the riches in the world.

Sandy, two years old, and Lila Mae

PREFACE

Salmagundi was written under the auspices of a grant sponsored by the San Leandro Public Library, which encouraged members to write about our lives. The published books are housed in the main library in a section called, The People's Library. This is one of a number of forward-thinking projects on the part of the library, which serves well as a community organization. Its programs reflect the voices, interests and needs of the local people.

When my mother was seventy-six, she wrote an autobiography that sparked many conversations between us about our time together. As accurately as possible, this book is an account of my childhood. While the text clearly states that I learned of the events from my mother, and I wrote the conversations as I remembered them, there are occasions in which I made up conversations to be what was reasonably said at the time. Some of the names are changed.

Thanks to Melissa Davis and Nils van Lingen, who did the design and art work, and to Ron Crowdy of Smartbomb Creative Studio for his photo composite of my mother and father. And thanks to the Arthur Leipzig Estate, Stephen Shames, the Charles Cushman Collection: Indiana University Archives, the Contra Costa Historical Society, and the Minnesota Historical Society, for permission to use their photos.

ST. PAUL, MINNESOTA

EARLY MEMORY

PALE, COLD LIGHT filtered through the window, casting shadows on the green and white linoleum, freezing us into place— me in my mother's arms, and my father, who stood with his face long and sour. His strong hands grabbed me by my arm and leg, snatched me from my mother's arms, and sent me flying. My little body skidded across the kitchen floor until I slammed into the wall. There I lay. It was winter. There was no sound. I could not make sense of what had happened to me, a baby, a little over a year old. My father stared belligerently into my mother's face.

"If you love me, you'll get rid of her!" he shouted.

*   *   *

That is the memory. What perplexes me is, I don't remember crying, or being scared, or even feeling threatened. Just that single flash of memory, the whoosh, the velocity of being yanked from my mother's arms and sliding across the linoleum. I have no other memories of my father when I was a baby. There are just a few from when I was older. They weren't good. Why wasn't I afraid of him? Why don't I remember? What follows is the rest of the story as I remember it, along with what my mother told me.

He repeated, "If you love me, you'll get rid of her!" My father pushed his face into my mother's. Her arms dangled at her sides, eyes sideways on me, her face still turned to meet his. How do you deal with a situation in which you find your husband is not the man you fell in love with? In that single second, my mother's world blew apart into a thousand smithereens. Already moving, my mother scooped me up from the floor.

*   *   *

The night before this incident my father had quarreled with my mother. "She's in the way," he stated. "I'm tired of her crying." He resented being relegated to taking care of me while my mother worked to earn money for the family.

Years later, I remember my mother talking about it, "Babies' bones are rubber. Sandy wasn't really hurt." She was talking to a friend in our apartment on E.70th Street in Manhattan while I played on the floor. I didn't like toys much, but I enjoyed listening to adults talk.

ST. PAUL, MINNESOTA

MY FATHER

MY FATHER, LATHROP EMMETT ROGERS, was a complex, destructive man. Frustrated by lack of opportunity, he suffered the ravages of racism poorly. Despite graduating at the top of his class with a B.A. in English literature, he could not secure a professional job. "Running the road," what the black man in the 1940s called serving as a waiter in the Pullman cars of railroad trains traveling to Chicago, the East coast and out West, was what my father eventually did. He was an angry man. So, my father kept his pride and didn't work after he and my mother married. He did drink.

Once, when I was seven years old, I visited my father in his tiny, dark, rented room in St. Paul.

"I can travel from St. Paul to Wyoming in one step. Can you do that?" His deep voice was directed at me, and he sat on his bed while I stood not two steps from the door. The room was small and shabby, with just room enough for a narrow bed and a chest of drawers.

A sliver of light from a small window high on the wall crossed in front of him, landing at my feet. I was intrigued and tried to imagine myself taking a giant step that would carry me halfway across the country. I am not sure now if he put those words into my mind, but the imagery was strong. Not knowing my father well— this

15

was one of a very few visits with him— I didn't respond.

"Look in my closet," he commanded. "The floor."

I took two steps to the narrow closet opposite his bed and pulled the door open. A light bulb with a string hanging down glowed yellow from above his very limited wardrobe, a couple of shirts, a few pairs of slacks. But the floor, glowing like a treasure, was covered in pure gold. Well, not gold really. The yellow light made the coins golden. The floor was covered in silver dollars. I immediately understood that they had fallen from his pockets when he hung up his pants. I don't think he told me then, but the silver dollars were tips he had earned while running the road.

My father patted the bed next to him. "Come sit down."

Moving slowly, stiffly, I sat next to him. I felt no connection to this man and was uncomfortable in his presence. My father boasted awhile about how lucky he was to travel out west and all over the country. As he talked, he inched closer to me on the bed. The room was dark and its shadows seemed to swallow us. I could smell alcohol on his breath.

I sat mute, not looking at him. His hand slid up my side and under my T-shirt, his fingers feeling the small nipples on my chest. I stood abruptly. "Let's go outside."

Amazingly, he rose with me and we left his room.

*   *   *

Almost forty-five years later, I sat in a student study team meeting with a number of teachers, the school psychologist, guardian, and the principal. We shared ideas about how to help a kindergarten girl who seemed to be having problems, both in and outside the classroom. We knew that the student suffered the disadvantages of poverty, but it was other aspects of her behavior that troubled us. She squirmed in her chair a lot— we suspected sexual abuse— and she had trouble focusing on what was taught. Further, her drawings gave a strong indication that she had been sexually molested. We were trying to put the disparate pieces of a puzzle together to form a plan to help the child.

As I sat in the conference room, a memory flashed in my mind of me sitting at a similar round table years ago with my own mother, my teacher, Ms. Scanlon, and the headmaster of my private school.

They were talking in hushed, serious tones as if I weren't there, and a crayon drawing of a naked man and woman lay on the table in front of them. I wondered at the crude figures, knowing that I had drawn them. However, I couldn't remember why or what I was thinking when I drew it, but I had the uncomfortable feeling that it was obscene. I didn't remember ever having seen a naked man or woman. *How did I know how to draw these people?* I had no memory of my mother and father living together.

I remembered sitting at the table in class as I was drawing. My eyes were focused on my picture, and my hand gripped a black crayon as I announced to my classmates, "Black is my favorite color."

The other students and the teacher paused for a moment as I made the assertion, listening. What did that mean? There were unmistakable breasts and a bush of hair on the woman and a penis on the man. There were no other colors in the drawing except for crude slashes of red, which suggested violence and blood. It was alarming, and I had forgotten it until that day forty-five years later in the after school meeting with the student study team.

The conversation in the meeting flowed around me while memories reeled in my head. I realized my father may have molested me when I was a baby in St. Paul. My mother left me with him while she went to work. It would have helped to explain why I had been such an emotional, hyperactive, insecure and demanding child.

After I became a seasoned teacher I realized that I was one of those children whom federal Title 1 legislation is designed to help through free lunch and academic support.

As an at-risk, poor, mixed-race kid, I was a walking statistic for failure and didn't know it. Yet, my memory of growing up, for the most part, was that of a happy, engaged child. How could I have been filled with such gusto and enthusiasm while living in such precarious circumstances? Sitting in that meeting as an experienced teacher of many years, I hadn't realized until that moment that I had been an at-risk child. I believe many at-risk children don't.

*   *   *

There is much more to the life of this complex man who was my father that I do not know. My mother thought he was born in 1910, to a poor, black family in their home outside of Wilkes Barre, Pennsylvania. There is no birth certificate or record of his birth.

Like many African Americans, my father's life was hard. His own father disappeared before he could remember him, and his mother died when he was six years old. My father was then shuffled around among relatives, who themselves were having trouble caring for their own families. He ran away from home when he was about twelve and made his way on the street. My mother told me that he lived by hanging around the back steps of brothels, doing favors and running errands. She said he probably suffered sexual exploitation during that time. He went to movies and taught himself to speak with a faux-British accent.

There are no records of my father having attended elementary or high school, and I know of no living relatives today. When Lathrop emerged at Macalester College in St. Paul, Minnesota, he was quite an urbane and cosmopolitan man. I have no idea how he gained admission.

When he graduated from college, the dean invited the six top students in the senior class to his house for dinner in honor of their academic achievement. My father, the only black student among them, was admitted at the side door and was served his meal at a table in the kitchen while the others were warmly greeted through the front door and enjoyed a formal dinner.

My father died an alcoholic in Chicago at the age of 50. He had a job pumping gas at a service station and lived in a rented room nearby. My mother said there were no personal effects in his room, no books, no papers, nothing to suggest what kind of person he was, except that he drank and smoked. He died alone, a two-dimensional figure, drained of depth and color. My mother drove down to Chicago from St. Paul, and saw to the arrangements for his burial in Chicago's potter's field. I was seventeen years old when he died.

*   *   *

EARLY MEMORY CONTINUED,

My mother was a quiet woman and a pacifist. She didn't respond to my father as he stood wavering before her that cold morning after he threw me across the kitchen floor. The vapors of alcohol swirled around them as they stood facing each other. The moment was invisibly violent. The night before she had put me in clean diapers and a jumper, swaddled me up tight, and put me in my crib to sleep as she always did. It should have been easy for my father to watch out for me. She put on her coat, kissed my father, and left to work the night shift at the Minnesota Mining and Manufacturing Company.

But babies don't always sleep through the night, and my father hated being a babysitter. "Get rid of her, or I will," he ordered, his voice a low growl hanging in the cold air. His complaint was a theme he had been harping on ever since my unplanned birth.

Tank house similar to Grandpa Porter's.
~Courtesy Contra Costa Historical Society

HAYWARD, CALIFORNIA

THE TANK HOUSE

YOU MIGHT AS WELL marry one a them niggers if you're gonna go out with that Italian boy," my grandfather offered as my mother was getting ready to leave.

And that is exactly what my mother did. She went out and married a black man, my father.

My Grandfather Porter, the son of Norwegian immigrants, had survived the Depression but was old now and afflicted with Parkinson's disease and alcoholism. His life's unfortunate events had caught up with him. Sometime after my mother graduated from Macalester in St. Paul, she and her sister, June, lived with him in a tank house[2] in Hayward, California. The house was located just off Hesperian Boulevard. The San Francisco Bay was nearby, not yet having been diminished by bay fill.

Grandpa Porter did not see himself as a racist.

"I just don't know any decent, upstanding Negroes," he declared.

Actually, Grandpa did not know any black people at all, but he did not let this interfere with his reasoning on the matter. They were talking about a date my mother was going on with an Italian boy she had known in high school. Her father's prescient injunction was delivered as she was getting ready to take the bus to class at the University of

---

[1] Tank house, a water tower placed high off the ground to provide water to a home or garden. Elevating the water tank insured water pressure.

California, Berkeley.

The bus ride took two hours, she told me, and wound its way on city streets mostly through fruit orchards. She was taking summer classes in a master's program in English literature.

Aunt June, Grandpa Reuben and Lila Mae

Lila Mae Porter and Lathrop Rogers
Photo composite by Ron Crowdy, Smartbomb Creative Studio

FALLING IN LOVE

While she was an undergraduate in St. Paul, my mother met the love of her life, Lathrop Emmett Rogers, one of the very few black men who attended Macalester College. Both were English majors and top students. He was three years ahead of her and eight years older. Lathrop was suave and spoke with precise diction, his rich vocabulary emerging from a languid mouth and a slow smile. His words drifted up through the smoke of his ever-present cigarette, his eyes squinting as if to consider. He emphasized his discourse with a sardonic tilt of the head, making my mother think he was thinking about her while his words spoke of something different. On the few occasions I saw him as a child, his diction fascinated me. I had never heard such an erudite speaker. I can still hear the way he pronounced my first name— "SUN-druh!"

My mother and father were united in the way young people are when they are newly politicized and fervently believe they can change the world. But they were alike in other ways, too. Both were children of the Depression and had grown up in poverty. Both lost their mothers when they were very young, and were farmed out to relatives. My mother attended six different kindergartens when she was five years old. Her father moved the family from St. Paul to Chicago to Beloit, Wisconsin, desperately trying to save the life of his wife, Mabel, who was dying from a sepsis resulting from appendicitis. My mother was four years old when she died. Penicillin was invented in 1928, too late for her. The difference between my mother and father's upbringing was that after staying with a number of relatives, my mother and her sister were loved and raised by their paternal grandmother, while my father was left to his own resources on the street.

My father attended Communist Party meetings, and my mother was against war, much less a second world war. Their friends were bohemians, intellectuals and true believers[2] In their zeal, they formed a commune, and rented a house together near Macalester College. Only the men slept in the house, though. The women couldn't actually be seen to stay overnight because it would have broken the bounds of propriety. However, my mother spent many evenings there talking late into the night, smoking cigarettes and discussing politics.

The commune created a worker's cooperative to help the people in the black community in St. Paul. It was sponsored by the Women's International League for Peace and Freedom and was housed at the Hallie Q. Brown Settlement House, which served the black community.

2 Eric Hoffer, a social philosopher, coined the term, *true believer*. He worked for a time as a Longshoreman. He studied fanaticism and mass movements like those led by Hitler and Stalin. Hoffer was born in 1898 in the Bronx, and was a professor at UC Berkeley during the time of the Free Speech Movement. The *True Believer* was published in 1951, and was still widely read when I read it in 1965 as a graduate student at UC Berkeley.

Later, when I was five, I attended Hallie's summer day camp and lived with Margaret's mother, Mrs. Williams. The workers' cooperative found jobs for the unemployed, distributed food, and helped families with housing. They were on fire and beautiful, talking all the time about how to help the down and out. This was not long after the Depression when people were still getting on their feet.

But something happened between my mother and father in St. Paul. Some kind of problem, and as a result my mother moved to California to think things through. She wasn't sure what to do with her life, so she enrolled in a master's program at the University of California, Berkeley.

That summer she discovered she was pregnant. It was July 1942.

Georgia Rogers

so, if i could . . .
i would whisper into my grandma georgia rogers' ear—
born not ten years after the end of the civil war—
i would say,

> *tell me*
> *tell me about things*

and grandma georgia rogers would roll her eyes up,
"Lawd, help me with this chile and her endless questions.
now, she wants to know about the beginning of things"

she grew quiet,
drew into herself, her cataracts tinting her eyes a bluish
cast
and I waited
leaned on the arm of her rocking chair, one foot on the
rocker,
pushing her back and forth
with my body and kind of resting against her.
I loved the smell of flour on her dress, pressed against my
cheek.

grandma georgia closed her eyes, sinking into memories
of when she was my age, seven
she became a little girl, herself
and, deep in thought,
addressed her grandma juba, my great grandma
who worked on the Rogers' slaveholder's plantation.

yes, these memories are passed on,
even as her grandma juba linked back to her mama, back,
back
to the dark days
when they were shipped to the colonies, cargo
rather than the proud sons and daughters of the Americas,
like the D.A.R.

I shivered, but I knew.
Lathrop Rogers, my father, was her son
And in his life he played out all the agony
and conflict
of the black man in America.

October 2015

NAME:	**Lathrop Rogers**
AGE:	**10**
BIRTH YEAR:	**1910**
BIRTHPLACE:	**Georgia**
HOME IN 1920:	**Cordele Ward 2, Crisp, Georgia**
RACE:	**Black**
GENDER:	**Male**
RELATION TO HEAD OF HOUSE:	**Son**
MARITAL STATUS:	**Single**
FATHER'S BIRTHPLACE:	**Georgia**
MOTHER'S NAME:	**Georgia Rogers**
MOTHER'S BIRTHPLACE:	**Georgia**

Record found on Ancestry.com, which suggests my father could have been born in Georgia.

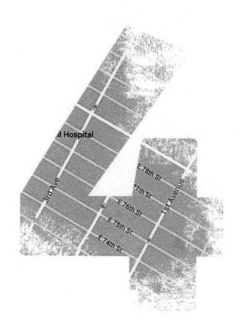

NEW YORK CITY

FLIGHT

THAT FATEFUL WINTER morning after my father threw me across the floor, he stumbled from the kitchen and fell into bed. Soon he was snoring in grumpy slumber, aided by the alcohol he used to keep on an even keel. My mother, stricken, became intensely focused. By then she had a pretty good understanding of the corrosive elements in her marriage, and she had grown more and more frightened that my father would fulfill his threat and actually kill me. It seems incredible that I can remember an incident from so long ago; perhaps it is the memory of what my mother told me.

My mother decided to run away from my father. She scooped me up from the floor and kissed me, and holding me close, grabbed a suitcase from the closet. She started throwing clothes in it. She didn't know what she was packing, underwear, diapers, dresses. She bundled me into a baby blue snowsuit that zipped from the ankle to the neck and tied a knit hat under my chin. She slid the hood of the snowsuit over my head. We were stepping into a snowy winter outside, temperatures sinking below freezing. She put on my little white high-top baby shoes and tied them. With suitcase and purse in one hand, and carrying me in her right arm like a bag of groceries, my mother fled the

Grand Central Station
Courtesy New York City Municipal Archives

flat they had been renting in the black neighborhood in St. Paul, Minnesota.

My mother took a bus and then a cab to the airport and purchased a one-way ticket to New York City. I immediately fell asleep as the plane climbed into the sky. My mother leaned back in her seat with a sigh. It was her first chance to relax since the whole horrible scene in the kitchen. She realized that in that one scintillating moment, her world had changed irrevocably. It was the defining moment of our lives.

We had to change planes in Chicago, but there was a terrible snowstorm and the flight was delayed. Finally, the airline offered to let her cash in her tickets so she could take a train to New York. My mother let me sleep on the bench next to her while she waited for the train. There was no money for a hotel or food. When it was time to board, she woke me, and in the commotion of gathering her suitcase and purse and picking me up, my mother did not notice that one of my shoes had fallen off. She would have to carry me all the rest of the way.

The train chugged through a snowstorm all through the night, and when we arrived in New York City, the streets were filled with snow and slush. My mother knew I couldn't travel in winter with a missing shoe, so she hauled me and her suitcase about nine blocks to Stern's department store on 42nd Street, where she bought me a new pair of shoes, even though she couldn't afford them. Then she slogged her way back through the snow to Grand Central Station, found a pay phone and called John Rue, one of her friends from Minnesota. He gave her directions from Grand Central Station to his apartment.

JOHN RUE

My mother met John Rue, a shy boy from a small town in southern Minnesota, when she was at Macalester College and he was attending the University of Minnesota. They became fast friends in their shared activities for world peace. They could have been mistaken for brother and sister; both were apple-cheeked, blue-eyed, blond young saplings. John was part of the mix of people who made up the commune they had formed to provide a work cooperative in St. Paul's black community.

My father, Lathrop Rogers, was part of the group of activist friends. They were very busy as they zealously pursued their goal of a more equitable society. I know from my own experience joining a commune when I was about the same age that a lot of the charisma that bound these people together was generated in the romance of their shared ideals. Fevered political passion sometimes overflows into romantic relationships, and this was the medium through which my mother met my father and fell in love.

John Rue was shy and reserved, highly intelligent and well read. He majored in music at the University, his goal to become a classical pianist. John didn't say much, but when he spoke, he did so with meticulously precise phrasing. When I was a child, I watched carefully the way he flicked the ashes from his cigarette. He closed his eyes, tilted his chin up and spoke with slow deliberation. John sat with a straight spine, his legs crossed gracefully at the knee and his arm cocked at the elbow, holding his cigarette. I loved the way he exhaled the cigarette smoke, turning his head to the side to avoid it, his eyes still closed.

I was born on John's birthday, April 5, 1943. My mother, swollen with pregnancy, threw a birthday party for John that night. Their political friends and members of the commune were at the apartment my mother and father now rented in St. Paul. Quite suddenly, my mother went into labor. She wasn't able to enjoy the party and was rushed to Maternity Hospital in Minneapolis to deliver her first child, me. From then on, John, my mother and I shared a kind of family tradition in which John and I celebrated our birthdays together. We did this every year until I moved to California in 1965.

John's plans to become a concert pianist came to an abrupt end when the U.S. entered World War II. John was a conscientious objector and assigned alternative service with the American Friends Service Committee, who sent him to

China to work for the Red Cross. However, the Communists threw John into prison, where he was incarcerated for five years. We don't know why he was thrown in jail, but it may have been because he was gay. He should have been safe in China, working under the auspices of the Red Cross.

While in prison, John slowly taught himself Mandarin by listening to the guards talk to each other and by reading the Chinese newspapers. Over the years, the guards conversed with him a bit, as well. When he was finally released and returned to America, John was fluent and literate in Chinese.

John's dream of becoming a classical pianist had been left far behind in an earlier time when he was young and innocent. When he returned to the United States he earned a PhD in political science from the University of Michigan. My mother typed his dissertation, and I also helped work on it by coding the research materials, quotes and references.

Because of his years in a Chinese jail, John became the leading authority in the United States on Chinese politics. He was the only American scholar at the time who could read the source documents in Chinese. He took a position as professor of political science at the University of Michigan and then at Stanford University. In fact, it was my visit to him and his family in Menlo Park that triggered my entry into graduate school at the University of California, Berkeley in 1965.

Nine years later, John visited my husband, Ed Arkin, and me when we were living in a commune called Synanon, in Marin County. John was delighted to see our newborn daughter, Cassidy, who was born on June 21, 1974. He was very unhappy and lonely at the time. His marriage had broken up and he was at sea emotionally. I don't think he had admitted to the world that he was gay; I certainly hadn't realized it as I was growing up, but it must have been a factor in the breakup of his marriage. John told me how unhappy he was, and we talked about his poetry. He was experimenting with a Chinese literary tradition of using specific words whose sound engenders wider concepts than the literal words in the poem. I urged him to move into Synanon. He was interested, but somehow just didn't do it.

Shortly after, I learned that John had committed suicide, and I felt I should have done more to help him. John was someone I had looked up to and relied on since I was an infant. I hadn't realized how lost he had become. His suicide was shocking and sad for all of us in our family. We each wondered if we could have done something to help him. Perhaps I should have tried harder to help John come into Synanon in 1974.

Years later, my sister Ann, who lives in St. Paul, was cleaning out her attic and came across a sheaf of typed papers. At first she thought it was a piece of our mother's writing, but upon reading the cover, she found it was a long poem titled, *A Reasonable Harmony, Reflections after the Battle at Chungmou*, North China, 1947. The dedication read, "To Lila Porter Rogers Pineles, one who loves."

As a kid, and without a father, I sometimes wondered why my mother didn't marry John. It was clear they enjoyed each other's company and were loyal to each other. They were a perfect match. However, John's being gay made that impossible.

There was more. After I left Synanon, remarried, and had two children, I went to visit John's ex-wife, Sally, at her home in Berkeley. The last time we had seen each other was when I visited them in Menlo Park in 1965. Before that, our two families had lived just blocks apart in SE Minneapolis near the University, and in the black community of St. Paul. When I was fifteen, Sally offered me twenty-five dollars to vacuum, dust, clean the bathroom and wash their kitchen floor on Sundays while they went to Quaker meeting. Recognizing the value of good wages, I told my Episcopalian priest that I no longer believed in God and went to work for the Rues.

Those many years later, Sally welcomed me to her home in Berkeley, and we spent the afternoon reminiscing and catching up. When I was about to leave, we stood in the doorway, saying our good byes. Suddenly, Sally said,

"You know your father buggered John, don't you?"

The comment struck me like a ball of lightning. I instantly understood that she meant my father had sodomized John. In those days, we did not talk openly about sexual matters. I thought, *How could she be so callous?* It seemed mean-spirited. I was shocked, hurt, confused and angry all at once.

I instantly realized my mother and John had *both* fallen in love with my father. It must have been heartbreaking for them to be in love with the same man. They each saw how my father hurt the other, and yet were hopelessly in love with the man themselves. I also understood how dark and malicious my father's motivations could be. Overwhelmed, I fled Sally's house and drove wildly home on Highway 580 to San Leandro.

Irrational as it was, I assumed the stigma of my father's actions, as I must have done unconsciously all my life, assuming the negative associations that went along with being black. It seemed inevitable that I be like him, since I was his flesh and blood, and I was a black child, more like him, I thought, than I was like my mother whom I idolized. I know now that I am very much like my mother. However, even with a little black blood in you, in America, a person is considered black, and I have always seen myself as black.

After putting the pieces of my mother's life together

and noticing the striking patterns playing out from hers to mine, I find I know so little, really, about her. Every new bit of information opens up new revelations and new understandings. Now my mother is gone, and I wish I could talk with her about the parallel patterns in our lives and the choices we made.

Margaret Williams,
Nursery school teacher, and Sandy,

SIMPLY KEEP WARM AND DRY

What followed when we arrived in New York was a wild time. John lived on the sixth floor of a tenement in the Bronx. It was snowing, and the roof leaked. There was water all over the floors, and the building superintendent, the super, always frugal, provided a minimum of heat through the radiators. I sat bouncing and squirming on my mother's lap during their conversation, and we were all wearing jackets and sweaters indoors because of the cold.

John and my mother talked earnestly, planning. How could she get a job? Applying for welfare or public assistance was out of the question. My mother was afraid the authorities would take me away from her and place me with a black foster family. In the '40s, it was believed black children were best raised in black families. My mother's family had urged her to put me up for adoption. Steadfast in her conviction to keep me, my mother had nothing more to do with her family. Such was the force of my mother's maternal instinct that she stuck it out and kept me. She was 27 years old.

John agreed that he would take care of me while she looked for a job and secured childcare. A series of misadventures followed. First, someone gave me some coins to play with and I swallowed a penny. My mother was alarmed about it, but didn't have the money to see a doctor or pay for an x-ray. Eventually nature took care of the problem. On another occasion they had friends over, and someone left a bottle of Mogen David wine on the kitchen table within my reach. Apparently, I drank some and got tipsy. Then my mother noticed that I had a suspicious rash. This time she took me to the doctor. I had come down with chickenpox. The doctor reassured her it was a normal childhood disease.

"Just keep her warm and dry," he advised, "and let it play itself out."

But that was impossible. I couldn't toddle around on John's wet floor, and his apartment was anything but warm. I literally spent the next few days on John's hip as he went about his day.

Then someone threw a lighted cigarette or somehow started a fire in the garbage chute that ran down the floors through the apartments. Soon, a fire was roaring up through the chute to the roof. The embers fell on the roof and burned a hole in our kitchen ceiling. My mother, John, and I huddled on the fire escape that evening, snow falling around us, waiting for the fire to be put out. The landlord refused to repair the hole in the roof until he got the insurance money, so now the apartment was really cold and very wet and unprotected from the winter weather, and I had chicken pox.

*   *   *

Margaret Williams,
Nursery school teacher, and Sandy.

My mother decided to stay with friends in Jamaica and Queens for a while as she continued to look for a job and childcare. She found a church charity that agreed to accept me in their nursery even though the minimum age was two years.

"Well, Mrs. Rogers, I sympathize with you," Sister Lucretia had said. "If you can get her toilet-trained, we will accept Sandy."

Incredibly, my mother toilet-trained me at eighteen months, which may explain my OCD tendencies today. I am sure there were accidents that the nuns forgave, but with childcare solved, my mother was able to take a job as a secretary in the office of the Polish government which was in exile in New York.

The man she worked for escaped Poland when the Red Army occupied it. Unfortunately, my mother could not understand her boss's halting English, and he, a somewhat autocratic man, could not understand why she didn't understand him. She ended up accepting a job as secretary to the National Committee for Conscientious Objectors of the American Civil Liberties Union. Roger Baldwin, the man who founded the American Civil Liberties Union, interviewed her. She earned thirty dollars a week. The job was exciting and stimulating, but it only lasted until May, 1945 when the Germans surrendered. That's when my mother got a job at the Lenox Hill Settlement House on

E.70th Street and enrolled me in the nursery school there. Margaret Williams was my teacher. Margaret was African-American, also from Minnesota, and about the same age. She and my mother immediately struck up a friendship. We moved into an apartment up the street from Lenox Hill not long after, and for a short while Margaret lived with us.

*   *   *

Queens

Lila and Sandy at the beach.

New York summers were beastly hot and humid. Buildings and skyscrapers captured the sun's heat during the day and trapped it in their cement corridors at night. There was no relief. To escape the sweltering heat, my mother took me to Jones Beach or Coney Island. I loved playing in the ocean waves, and my mother would try to get a suntan, a nearly impossible aspiration, with her fair, white Norwegian skin. She often came home from these trips sun sick and nauseated and asked me to put ice cubes on the sunburns on her shoulders.

We traveled to Coney Island by bus and by subway, and made a day of it. On one occasion when we were returning home from the beach, a lady on the bus bawled out my mother.

"You ought to be careful. Keep your baby out of the sun. She's badly sunburned." She scowled at my mother in disapproval.

The lady did not know I was black.

My mother did not know how to respond. If she explained that I was part Negro, she would invite more criticism— what kind of white woman raises a colored child? She already knew the answer: a prostitute. She remained stoic and kept her thoughts to herself. But I vividly remember her talking about it afterwards with Margaret, my nursery school teacher.

Sandy playing on Lenox Hill rooftop playground

5

NEW YORK CITY

Arthur Leipzig, East River Jumpers, 1948
© Estate of Arthur Leipzig, Courtesy of Howard Greenberg Gallery, New York

311 E. 70TH STREET

SOON WE WERE LIVING in our own walkup on the fifth floor of a tenement in Manhattan. Our building was located on E.70th Street, between First and Second Avenue, a couple blocks from the East River, where the local kids used to swim during the hottest days of summer, despite common knowledge that the river was polluted. My memories of that time were happy, even though life must have been difficult for my mother.

When we went shopping, she carried the groceries in one arm and dragged me along with her free hand. We did a lot of walking, and by the time we headed home I was often tired and reluctant to walk. My mother had to drag me as I hung back on her hand. When we went to the laundromat, my mother lugged the basket of wet laundry home and carried it up six flights of stairs to the roof where she hung it out to dry. At the time I had no true grasp of the stress my mother must have dealt with to get an apartment, work full time, arrange childcare, and build a life for us.

But life in New York City was exciting. New York was not only my world, it was the center of the world. Traveling on the subway and bus gave me a clear sense of the geography of Manhattan Island, with Central Park running down its center. This world was filled with tall buildings. The skyscrapers made it famous.

Sandy with friends on roof top playground,
Lenox Hill settlement house

Down the block was Lenox Hill, the settlement house where I attended nursery school. In a photograph taken on the rooftop playground of Lenox Hill, I'm the kid in the middle, four years old. Some have asked if I were the little girl on the left. They may have presumed the middle child was a boy because of the way I was dressed. My mother sewed all my clothes, including my coat, and bought boys' lace-up shoes for me because they were sturdier than girls' shoes. My hair was fine and kinky and did not get combed every day. I cried when the brush pulled at my tangles, and often, in the rush of getting to work, my mother just smoothed it over and took me to nursery school hoping I was presentable.

My mother's Norwegian upbringing was austere, and did not approve of prettying up little girls. When I went to middle and high school, she refused to let me wear lipstick or earrings. Of course, the minute I turned the corner from our house on my way to school, I would sneak on my secretly purchased pale, pink lipstick.

Lenox Hill was unusual because its playground was on the roof. From it I could see the city and the grid of streets that defined it. I remember corridors of sky when I walked on the sidewalk and was later impressed by the contrast of a limitless horizon when I lived in Minnesota. The Lenox Hill Settlement House is still in operation today.

When I was a child, I had a recurring nightmare

about a reservoir that I could see from the rooftop playground. I am not sure now if there really was an open reservoir in Manhattan; it may have been part of a conversation I overheard. I was captivated by the concept of a deep pool and thought of its sparkling, blue water when I took my baths in the double utility sink in our apartment.

In my dream I played on the shallow steps that led down, maybe two hundred feet, to a drain in the bottom. I splashed and played in the water and as time passed, I became more and more comfortable, enjoying the water and venturing farther and farther down the steps and deeper into the water. Little by little, I moved away from the safety of the top steps at the surface of the reservoir. Suddenly, the water would slowly began to swirl, creating a funnel and with a heavy tug, pulled at me toward the drain at the bottom. I dreaded being sucked down into the vortex. Dreams about water still haunt me today. I think the imagery is about venturing into life, taking risks, but being careful not to get sucked in.

*   *   *

Tenement, New York City. ~Charles W. Cushman Collection:
Indiana University Archives. Image #P02689, "Street scene below Brooklyn
Bridge Lewis St. north from DeLancey. October 4, 1942."

The reddish-brown, brick apartment buildings on our block all looked the same, with five steps leading up to a heavy door that opened into a hallway with mailboxes, and a stairway to the upper floors. In front of each building was a "stoop," on which people hung out and talked. A fire escape graced the front of each tenement. In the sweltering heat of summer my mother and I often sat on the fire escape outside our living room window and had a picnic. We also spread a blanket on the roof and sunbathed, pretending we were at the beach. At night I remember the plaintive notes of a sax as a man sitting on a kitchen chair played jazz riffs two roofs over. I loved New York City.

Coming home from school, I sometimes entered the wrong building by mistake. We lived on the top floor, and I would climb partway up a flight of stairs before becoming worried and uneasy. *Where was I? What had happened to my house?* The most frequent giveaway that I was in the wrong building was the smell. Each tenement had its own distinctive odor. Mine held the redolence of boiled cabbage, brisket, and soup. I saw the world as unpredictable and was young enough to believe my building might have disappeared entirely. Realizing I had entered the wrong building, I would quickly descend the stairs and pay close attention until I found the correct building.

*   *   *

At the grocery my mother bought oleomargarine. We used it instead of butter, which was expensive. The oleo, as my mother called it, looked like lard, white and congealed, in a small cellophane-wrapped package. On top, in the middle, kind of like a belly button, was a small, round, packet of orange dye that my mother would pierce and then mash into the oleo so that the whole thing took on the rich, yellowy color of butter. I enjoyed watching her go through the process of turning the margarine into oleomargarine.

*   *   *

Once I started first grade, there were long periods after school when I was on my own until my mother came home from work. At this time I played with the kids on the street. We played pretend games, making up long stories of the quality of today's soap operas, full of drama, danger, pride and confrontation. Each story went on for days. We gathered in the same place, by some trash cans or the side railing of a stoop, and talked excitedly as we got started. It was the location of our gathering point that reminded us where we had left off the day before. I remembered this later as a teacher, that learning is geographic as well as physical and mental.

As kids, our values were shaped by movie stars like Humphrey Bogart, Roy Rogers, and John Wayne and emerged in our dramas, whether we were playing gangsters, princess, or cowboys. Courage, valor, bravery, and standing up to someone, was what we what we wanted to act out in our scenarios.

As six o'clock drew near, my neighborhood friends, one by one, were called home for dinner, to do homework or chores. I then explored my building and the other buildings on the street. Sometimes I walked around the block or walked up as far as 78th Street. I stayed on one side of the street so that I could find my way back. Eventually, the long shadows of evening crept over the neighborhood as the hour grew late. The other kids had already been called in to supper, and I reluctantly went inside. I didn't have a key to the apartment.

By now, my mother worked on the West Side and didn't get home until late. She took the subway and a cross-town bus from the Hudson Guild, a settlement house by the docks on the Hudson River. *East side, west side, all around the town*[3], the song would go. The west side was more glamorous with its docks, shipping and ocean liners.

As the day petered out and I ran out of things to do on the street, I would trudge up the five flights of stairs to

[3] Lawler, Charles. Lyrics by James W. Blake. *The Sidewalks of New York*, once considered an anthem for the city. Camden, New Jersey. Victor Recordings, 1894.

my floor. I sat there on the top step gazing down through the crisscrossing banisters into the stairwell, waiting to see my mother's hand on the railing. The stairwell was a deep space filled with brown color reflecting from the walls and lit in spots by warm, yellow incandescent lights. I thought about its depth, practiced trotting down the stairs in a small, nonchalant gallop, and slid down the banisters. I was fascinated by the structure of this deep, narrow reservoir of shadowy space. At these moments, time seemed to stand still in a dark well of silence, and I felt incredibly alone.

*   *   *

There were four apartments on each floor of our building and an old-fashioned, water-closet-style bathroom shared by the families, sat in the middle, facing the stairs. The dark bathroom had a narrow, hallway, leading back to the toilet. It was not heated. The toilet itself seemed a huge, porcelain cavern with a big wooden toilet seat. If I wasn't careful, my little bottom slid through and slipped into the cold water deep inside. The toilet bowl seemed enormous. When I finished, I stood and pulled a long chain that hung from a tank near the ceiling that released huge rushes of water clamoring down into the toilet. It was impressively loud and a little scary, and I tried to run out of the bathroom before all the water flushed through for fear it might overtake me.

We had a three-room, railroad-style apartment. The living room facing the street, the kitchen was in the middle, and my tiny bedroom was in the back with its one window facing the building next door. You walked in from the hall into the kitchen, with its linoleum floor, gas stove, and shoulder-high refrigerator. The little stove and oven was almost the size of a woman's dressing table. The oven did not provide reliable heat, which accounted for my mother's sigh of relief when her cakes and pies came out all right. We sat at a small table in the center for our meals. Sometimes while my mother cooked, she placed a bowl of milk on the floor under the table and I played puppy, yipping and lapping up the milk. I begged her for a pet dog, but, of course, pets weren't allowed.

On the left as you entered the kitchen, was a double utility tub of dark stone with its center divider removed. This was our bathtub. Next to it was a shallow sink in which my mother washed dishes and vegetables. A white-enameled tin lid covered the tub. My mother sewed curtains for all the windows out of white, sheer fabric. She also sewed my clothes, including my coats. At the front was our living room. It had two windows facing the street and a fire escape outside. In between the two windows was a drop-leaf table I used to climb to practice my smiles in the mirror hanging above it. My mother slept in the living room on what she called a "studio couch," which was actually a rollaway bed covered with a madras spread.

Across from my mother's bed was a large console radio and record player that stood four feet high. I used to sit cross-legged on the floor in front of it and listen to radio programs, staring at a flickering gold light at the center of its dial and imagining Jack Benny and his cast—Mary Livingston, Rochester, and Phil Harris, reading their scripts. We listened to the *Green Hornet, Hopalong Cassidy,* and mysteries on the radio, conjuring up the imagery as we followed along. My mother also tuned in fairy tales on Saturday mornings.

Her treadle sewing machine sat in the darkest corner of the living room in front of an angled window that opened to an open shaft that separated our building from the one next door. On this inside corner wall, the small window did not let in much light. An old Jewish lady who lived in the building next to us sometimes handed me buttered matzo crackers through the window. To me, she seemed to live in some other world, perhaps from one of Andersen's fairy tales, because we each entered our apartments from different buildings, and I never saw her except on those occasions when her smiling wrinkled face appeared, talking in a friendly Yiddish. Each of these areas of the living room was like a separate room to me.

The only other furniture in the living room was a

couple of straight-backed chairs and a bookcase. We had no phone or television. My mother's black vinyl record albums were lined up against a wall on the floor, classical, jazz, the Weavers and folk music.

To the right, as we entered the apartment, was my bedroom. It was small, with a narrow window that faced the building next door. Very little sunlight made its way in. My bed, chest of drawers and doll carriage crowded the small space. I routinely collapsed the bed by climbing on top of the chest of drawers, jumping off and bouncing on the mattress. My mother would say, "Oh, dear!" and figure out how to put the bed back together again.

BEDTIME

"Mommy, Mommy, please bring me a drink of water!"

My mother had early decided that God created bedtime so that parents could have some peace and quiet. But as so often happens, things do not always follow God's plan. Every evening she bathed me, put me in my pajamas and read to me before putting me to bed. She read the classics, Winnie the Pooh and Christopher Robin, the fairy tales of the Brothers Grimm and Hans Christian Andersen, *East of the Sun and West of the Moon*, poetry, and stories from mythology. I curled up against her and lost myself in another world as she read aloud, the faint smell of cigarettes wafting over me from her breath. I cuddled into her and tried to prolong the reading as long as I could.

We talked about what was happening, whether or not Eeyore was rude, or Piglet's feelings were hurt. As a young child, I sought to make meaning of my life. After reading aloud to me, my mother and I had many long conversations in which she tried to answer my questions about good and evil and happiness and justice. Why aren't bad people ugly and good people beautiful? If you are good, shouldn't you be beautiful, too? How can you tell a person is bad if he is handsome?

Our conversation inevitably turned to God and Jesus Christ, and we also talked about eternity, time and space, topics most of us grapple with as adults. I tried to understand in practical terms what, "forever and ever, Amen," from the Lord's Prayer meant, and my mother was exultant as she told her friends, how I told her, "I know how it can go on forever and ever. Maybe the end is stuck on to the beginning." My mother was proud that I had some concept of infinity. Finally, she would insist that I go to sleep, and then the tossing around would start. A hyperactive kid, I never seemed to be ready to fall asleep at bedtime.

My mother's clothes hung in my closet, and, after she tucked me in bed, I sometimes stared at the closet door, which was usually left partially open. What if there were monsters in the closet? I was too frightened to get out of bed and shut the door. Sometimes I drifted into a wide-awake slumber and actually saw little green monsters playing on the scarves and belts hanging from the doorknob, and then I woke up screaming.

My mother consoled me, "There are no monsters. There, there, go to sleep."

Then followed the water fetching game, which usually lasted until about 10:00 o'clock when I finally fell asleep.

MALLADO

My best friend, Sofia Gambino, lived downstairs on the second floor. She and I were the only girls our age on the block, and wonder of wonders, we lived in the same building. We immediately became best friends. This meant sitting on the front stoop and discussing all the ways that we were really sisters. This is when I realized that despite the fact that my mother was white and I was brown, people expected members of a family to look alike. We sat side by side and talked as I scratched my arm, crazing a white trail of dry skin and drawing designs on my forearm.

Sofia touched my arm, "Look, it's white. Do you think your whole skin could turn white if you scratched it enough?" It seemed a crazy idea to me, I scratched a little more, not sure how to keep the whitish tinge.

Sofia asked, "How did you get that way?"

"I dunno." Then I added, "I'm mallado," (mulatto), the word suddenly coming to me from a conversation I had overheard my mother having with a friend. "Mallado is half white and half Negro," I continued matter of factly, not really knowing what "Negro," was except that it involved some kind of apologetic association with people who have dark skin.

"Do you think you can ever become white like me?" Sofia asked.

"No, I can't." I had already thought that one through. I had always wanted soft bangs like the ones that framed my best friend's face. I longed to be able to execute a nonchalant shake of my head to slide the bangs out of my eyes. Sofia was my age, but much smaller than I. She had blue eyes and blond hair that hung to her shoulders. There were further impediments to my appearance: I was tall for my age, my hair was done in two, unglamorous braids, and I wore glasses. There was little chance I could present the same lovely, sweet appearance as my best friend. When we played pretend games I was often cast as the Indian or the robber, never the princess. However, what I lacked in a traditional sense of being pretty I made up for in being bright and loquacious.

Racism is taught rather than intuited, Sofia and I

had no understanding of prevailing attitudes toward people of color. In the Italian and German neighborhood where we lived, called the Bund section, some of the families had been sympathetic to Mussolini and Hitler in the Second World War.

Sofia's big brother, Sonny, was sixteen. He spent most of his free time on the street trying to look tough and running errands for the Gambino Family. He wanted to be a big shot. I remember one of the many times that Sofia had gotten permission from her mother for me to eat dinner with them. I loved having dinner with their big family. Mrs. Gambino served each of us a plate with a piece of white bread in the center swimming in gravy. So rich and tasty! My mother would not buy white bread. She said it was unhealthy and she baked her own whole wheat bread which I was deeply ashamed of.

As we dove in, Sonny asked his mother, "Why do you let a nigger come in the house?"

Curious, Sofia and I looked at the adults at the table to see what they would say. What was he talking about? Sofia's mother looked embarrassed. She said, "Not now. She's just a little girl and a friend of Sofia's." That was the end of it.

That night after I trudged up the flights of steps to my apartment, I asked my mother, "What is a nigger?" She became immediately concerned and asked me where

I had heard it. After I explained, she ended the discussion by saying it was not a very nice word to use. However, her evident discomfort told me much more about the power of this word than her explanation.

It was shortly after that my mother managed to get a scholarship for me to attend a private school sponsored by the Episcopal church we attended. Some years later, I remember my mother saying, "I couldn't put her in the public school on the corner. I was scared to death how the neighborhood kids would treat Sandy." I was the only black kid on the block.

ALL THE ICE CREAM YOU WANT

"What?" Her voice veered sharply, like a knife carving an apple. The nice lady was looking at me, an eager, scruffy-brown, talkative child. Her eyes went wide and her eyebrows rose, as if lifting her lids would make my words clearer to hear. She sat facing my mother and me as we hurtled on the IRT subway careening uptown. But it was not the screeching howl of our transit that had taken her aback. It was this skinny little kid sitting up on the edge of the seat, eying her expectantly, waiting for a response.

"I have overactive sebaceous glands," I announced matter of factly, poorly masking my pride in this technical diagnosis. "The doctor said."

The lady remained mute, her eyes slid to my mother sitting next to me. Clearly, she did not understand.

"I hafta get my tonsils out," I added, helping her out. The train rocked from side to side as it screamed along the track to a stop barely a mile from our apartment on E.70th Street.

It was 1948, and I was five years old. I had recently suffered a series of chronic sore throats and earaches. My mother sent me to school on those mornings when I woke up sick and crying because she couldn't afford to take off work and had no one to care for me if I stayed home. It was a situation I later recognized as an educator in the public schools. My mother counted on the teacher to send me to the nurse's office to lie down. After several occurrences, however, the nurse had a talk with my mother and explained that she ought to take me to a doctor. It was the same teacher who alerted her later that year that I needed glasses. These are the unheralded, but needed functions a school can provide to a poor neighborhood.

The doctor poked his otoscope in my ear twisting it this way and that. I could feel his breath on my cheek as he breathed noisily through his nose. Finally, he looked up at my mother.

"There's a lot of wax buildup in there, part of an ear infection. Overactive sebaceous gland." He straightened, patting my knee. "I must tell you, it's time to take her tonsils out."

He turned to me, all charm, peering through his sparkling glasses, "How would you like to eat all the ice cream you like?"

My eyes grew wide in happy anticipation, not certain he meant it. The doctor nodded, "It's a tradition. When you get your tonsils out, you get to eat as much ice cream as you want. It makes your sore throat feel better."

I was all for it.

I looked around the office while the doctor and my mother talked, my legs swinging back and forth where I sat on the examination table. I could see into the windows of the red brick building across the street, and outside the traffic honked and squeaked in a dull roar, like a flock of pigeons under a blanket.

"I can't afford— " my mother ventured.

"Don't worry," the doctor interrupted. "Lenox Hill Hospital takes charity cases who qualify. They'll do the surgery on Sandy at no cost to you."

"That'd be wonderful!" my mother breathed in relief. She looked away in embarrassment. She was a proud, independent woman.

Within the week she and I were riding the IRT again from our apartment up to E.77th and Lexington Avenue. The hospital was situated between 76th and 77th and took up the entire block, bounded by Park Avenue on one side and Lexington on the other. The area around midtown Manhattan was familiar to me. I attended school on 5th Avenue off E.70th Street, opposite Central Park where we spent time exploring and visiting the lake and the Central Park Zoo. The Metropolitan Museum of Art and the Natural History Museum nearby were also regular haunts of my mother and me. These were places tourists came to New York to visit, but my mother and I considered them part of our neighborhood.

I had no idea what I was in for.

Built in 1857, Lenox Hill Hospital was originally called the German Hospital. Its mission was to serve the German families in the Bund section of Manhattan, regardless of race or creed. Towards the end of the First World War, however, with anti-German sentiment running high, its name was changed to Lenox Hill Hospital.

The five-story building reminded me of the dark, massive orphanage where the little girls lived in the story, Madeline, by Ludwig Bemelmans. My mother had read the book to me before bedtime many times. Published just four years before I was born, the popular book was considered a modern classic. I liked the story about the little girls who lived in an orphanage and went about Paris walking in two straight lines. They belonged to a place and were happy, and they lived in a big house where they were well taken care of. My nursery school, Lenox Hill Settlement House, down the street from our apartment, doubled as my home, too, filled with childcare workers who served government-ration saltine crackers and butter. I was a kid who longed for a home and family and took comfort in any reasonable facsimile of one.

I was admitted to the hospital, dressed in a white hospital gown, and prepared for surgery. I still hadn't caught on that I would undergo anesthesia or that my tonsils would actually be surgically removed. I was simply told, "You will go to sleep, and when you wake up, you won't have those pesky tonsils any more, and you can have all the ice cream you want to eat."

It was strange going into surgery, and I didn't want to be separated from my mother, but so much was happening, I didn't protest. Not knowing to be fearful, I was full of questions, asking about the rolling gurney, making friends with the nurses, and noting the lights in the hallway, until the ether put me under.

Before I knew it, I woke up in a hospital bed in a cavernous dark room. My mother was sitting beside me. The long room had a row of beds facing each other on opposite walls. At one end, the nurses in white uniforms that wafted like curtains sailed in and out in an unending flow of wordless efficiency.

I felt awful.

I started to cry. "What happened?" I croaked to my

mother, but couldn't say more. My throat was too sore to talk. She shifted in her chair and looked uncomfortable. I realize now she must have felt guilty, using the succession of ruses she had to get me to submit to surgery.

"Would you like some ice cream?"

Soon the ice cream came. It was French vanilla, which tasted bitter to my childish palette, more used to the sweetness of plain vanilla. Actually, it tasted like medicine and had a terrible aftertaste. And it hurt to swallow. I spat it out.

I had been bamboozled. What was the use of all the ice cream you could eat if it tasted awful and your throat was too sore to swallow? I looked at my mother with baleful eyes. She had let me down.

But there was a further betrayal. After a while, my mother stood up and drew her coat on, "I have to go," she said. "Visiting hours are over."

What? My mother is going to leave me here? My eyes darted around. The room was filled with darkness punctuated by yellow halos from the small lights over each bed. I was suddenly frightened.

"You can't leave me!" I protested. Sobbing, I clutched at her sleeve, as my mother patiently pulled her hand from mine.

"I have to," she replied. "I can't stay here, and tomorrow, I have to go to work. It'll only be three more days," she coaxed. "Then you can come home on the weekend and finish getting well there."

I can't describe the sadness and desolation that overcame me. I was just a little girl all by myself in a huge hospital room filled with beds and people I didn't know. It was eerily quiet, not a jolly place. I slid down under the covers and pulled the clean, starched sheets up to my chin, and gazed around me. The words from Madeline's story came unbidden, *Mrs. Clavel woke up in the night and said, 'Something is not right.'* She immediately rushed through the halls and found Madeline, who, it turned out, needed an appendectomy.

The story now held special resonance for me. Madeline's experience sustained me for the days while I got well enough to go home and back to school. I spent much of the time sleeping, but when I was awake, I pretended I was the little girl in that story.

And I had all the ice cream I wanted to eat.

In an old house in Paris that was covered with vines
Lived twelve little girls in two straight lines
In two straight lines they broke their bread
And brushed their teeth and went to bed.
They left the house at half past nine
In two straight lines in rain or shine-
The smallest one was Madeline [4]

[4] Bemelmans, Ludwig. Madeline. New York: Simon and Shuster, 1939.

MY MOTHER'S FRIENDS

Far from the posh luxury apartments that line the streets of mid-Manhattan today, in the late 1940s, my neighborhood was a teeming cauldron of immigrants. Anti-war sentiment was strong, as was the mafia and the exigent forces of poverty. Everyone talked about how to make it big in America and what we would do if we found a hundred dollars. "It's a free country," was a catch phrase and its implications occupied our imaginations.

My mother may have been one of a few intellectuals to move into the neighborhood. She also stood out as a single white mother of a black child. She was a curiosity, a pacifist sympathetic to political leftists, many of whom were communists. The leftist movement was rooted in civil rights issues, which McCarthy would soon try to quash in his hearings in 1954. The hearings demonized communists, and their influence extended well into the sixties.

I remember a refugee from Czechoslovakia, Alex, who came to our apartment on occasion. My mother's friends held him in hero status because he had managed to escape the Nazis when the Germans occupied Czechoslovakia. Unlike today, refugees from tyranny were eagerly offered asylum in the U.S., respected for their courage and given a warm welcome.

Every once in awhile my mother invited her friends

over. She cooked vegetables and spaghetti and baked a cake. It was a miracle if the cake turned out well because our oven was small and irregular. On those occasions our little three-room flat was filled with artists and dissidents from all over the world. I remember a Sikh cooking Indian food with curry he brought from his mother's kitchen in Delhi. There was much laughter, music, Chianti, cigarette smoke, and voluble conversation. Opera played wildly, and artists, sculptors, and photographers discussed their work and its relevance to the exciting new age unfolding around them. America, New York City, was an exciting place.

Sometimes I modeled for a painting class. My mother may have been paid $25 per hour for the job. When the artists took a break I walked around the room and looked at the portraits of me on the easels. I was astounded at the myriad versions of myself. Some portrayed me as a dark pickaninny with tight, curling braids, and others as a comely Caucasian child with pecan-colored skin.

At home, my mother often played opera and classical music on the record player. She had a collection of Decca records including George Shearing, Billie Holiday, the Ink Spots, Nat King Cole, the Weavers and classical music. Sometimes we danced down the length of the apartment to the lively beat of *The Patty Cake Polka*. We took the waltz position and bounded from the living room through the kitchen, into my room and back again.

We sang *Marching to Pretoria* together, a cheerfully sung, but sad, satiric song about a forced 1,000-mile march of blacks to Pretoria, South Africa. Josef Marais and Rosa de Miranda popularized the people's version of the British Boer War with this song. He was South African, and Miranda, born in Amsterdam, was a Dutch translator. They met in New York City in the early '40s.

My mother also taught me to hear the little bird twittering and the heavy, ominous footsteps of the giant wolf in Prokofiev's *Peter and the Wolf.*

THE ROSENBERGS

One of the political causes my mother's friends rallied around was the case of Julius and Ethel Rosenberg. One night, late, after everyone left a gathering at our apartment, my mother came into my bedroom to settle me in. I was a hyperactive kid, and although she put me to bed at 7:00 every night, I rarely fell asleep until late into the evening, especially on a night when the apartment was filled with interesting people laughing, smoking cigarettes, drinking cheap Chianti, and having a good time. One of the records my mother played during the evening was Billie Holiday. I remembered the song, *"Strange Fruit."*

Southern trees bear a strange fruit,
Blood on the leaves and blood at the root,
Black bodies swinging in the southern breeze,
Strange fruit hanging from the poplar trees.[5]

I wondered about the lyrics. "Why do you like that song, Mommy?"

She stubbed out her cigarette in an ashtray by my bed, "It's just beautiful, that's why."

Privately, I couldn't agree. Billie Holiday sounded groggy, sad and slow, lost in a reverie that underlay the simple lyrics. Of course, Holiday was often high on heroin, which may have accounted for some of the soulfulness and grogginess in her voice. I didn't realize that the strange fruit hanging from the tree was a black man lynched in the South, but while I didn't know what specific sadness Billie Holiday expressed, I felt it. What I caught as a percipient seven-year old was the aching sorrow in the melody, and I wondered why my mother and all those people embraced it.

I also didn't know one more interesting thing. *Strange Fruit* was actually written by a white man, Abel Meeropol, a teacher at Dewitt Clinton High School in the Bronx, the same high school my stepfather, Jack Pineles, whom I hadn't met yet, had attended. How my mother met Jack, her second husband, is another story.

[5] Meeropol, Abel. Bitter Fruit. New York Teacher, January, 1937.
© Teachers Union, Local 5, American Federation of Teachers 15788, 15789.

In 1939, Abel Meeropol was a conscientious young teacher concerned about racism in America. He was politically active and attended communist party meetings. This was not as shocking then as it became during the McCarthy hearings later. My father had also attended communist party meetings in Minnesota. It was where intellectually awake people gathered to discuss a new social order and figure out their role in it.

America was transforming itself right under everyone's nose, harvesting the energy of the industrial age—railroads, electricity, cars, assembly line manufacture—and combining it with the power of information to create a new, idealistic day in America.

My mother's friends had no riches, no property. Their power resided in their ability to share information about oppression all over the world, from the Nazis in the Second World War, to the Soviet invasion of Czechoslovakia in 1948. It was a time without Twitter, the Internet, blogs and instant online reportage of atrocities; yet, people knew what was happening. Many had come to New York City as refugees and were firsthand witnesses to oppression of all kinds, in Hungary, India, South Africa and Europe. They talked eagerly about the new world they were building. They were young then, but didn't know it. It was an exhilarating time.

One day, Abel Meeropol saw a photograph in a

newspaper of a lynching in the South. He was profoundly affected by it and couldn't get it out of his mind. He decided to tape the photograph of the lynching to the back wall of his classroom as a reminder while he taught and appreciate the contrast between the innocence of his students and the hideous oppression of black men. Racial oppression broke his heart, and this is what moved him to write, "Bitter Fruit." The poem was recognized by his colleagues as a powerful statement and printed in the teachers' union publication.

Meeropol was also an amateur composer. He set the words of his poem to music and played it for a club owner in Harlem. The name was changed slightly, and the owner invited Billie Holiday to sing it in his bar. Her soulful rendition of *Strange Fruit* catapulted her to widespread recognition, and the song became the banner of anti-discrimination in political activity.

What a fascinating juxtaposition: *Strange Fruit*, a song about the lynching of a black man in the South, was actually written by a white Jewish guy from the Bronx.

I learned something else that night as my mother was trying to coax me to sleep. I was troubled by another thing and continued asking questions.

"Why was everybody talking about the Rosenbergs, Mommy?" I was really leading up to questions about the children.

She responded vaguely, "Oh, the Rosenbergs were

a married couple who were wrongfully arrested as spies for the Soviet Union."

Later I learned that their case was at the center of a political battle between liberals and radicals on one side and anticommunists on the other. McCarthyism held such a strong influence that years later, when I was hired as a fifth grade teacher in California, I was asked to sign a loyalty statement stating that I was "not now nor never had been a member of the Communist Party."

I wish now that I had asked my mother more about the Rosenbergs. Knowing that they had children, two boys, had piqued my interest. My mother told me the boys were about my age, and I wondered about them. I had always wanted siblings, a complete family with a father, brothers and sisters, a piano, and a dog, and they had a complete family. Except, the Rosenberg family was breaking up. Although I probably did not express this to my mother at the time, I wondered what would happen to their children if the Rosenbergs went to jail. She mollified me gently with as much information as a seven-year-old needed to know and stayed with me until I fell asleep.

Years later I found out that the Rosenbergs had been executed as spies. Apparently, only Julius was guilty, and to this day their sons protest their mother's innocence. In Minnesota, when I was a teenager, the activities of the Sobel Committee were a commonplace in our lives. Morton

Sobel was also convicted of espionage and was sentenced to 30 years in prison, but at the time, my mother believed he was innocent. However, he eventually admitted his guilt in 2008.

Listening to a segment on NPR, I was surprised to learn that Abel Meeropol, the same man who had written, *Strange Fruit*, had adopted the two boys, Michael and Robert, who were orphaned when their parents were executed in 1953.

NEW YORK CITY

Popular song we sang as kids, typifying the spirit of New York City, sung in a lilting waltz time:

Sidewalks of New York

> *East Side, West Side, all around the town,*
> *Tots sing, "Ring around Rosie, London Bridge is*
> *   falling down.*
> *Boys and girls together, me and Mamie O'Rourke,*
> *We tripped the light fantastic on the sidewalks*
> *   of New York.*
> ~ Composed by James W. Blake and Charles B. Lawlor

I knew from an early age that New York was an extraordinary place. New York was in fact a world-class city. It was the center of the arts, music, fashion, culture, commerce and diplomacy of the time. I remember when my mother went to see the musical, *South Pacific* on Broadway. She was thrilled by the performance and described how Mary Martin had actually shampooed her hair on stage as she sang, "I'm gonna wash that man right out of my hair." My mother also told me about New York as we traveled around on the subway and the bus. She took me to Central Park, the Museum of Natural History, the Museum of Modern Art and the Public Library, and in November we walked through Central Park to watch the Macy's Thanksgiving parade.

Sometimes, when my mother got her paycheck, we would go on a "binge." We went to Chock Full O'Nuts and she ordered a cream cheese sandwich on date-nut bread, which we shared. There were bits of walnuts in the cream cheese, and the sandwich was rendered sweet by the dark bread. She also took me to the Horn and Hardart Automat, where she bought a piece of pie set in a little box behind a glass door. She deposited nickels, pulled the little chrome knob and took out a small plate with the slice of pie on it. Then she would buy a cup of coffee. We sat at the counter and shared the pie and looked out the glass windows at people passing on the street.

My mother enrolled me in a painting class at the Guggenheim Museum when I was five, and we often had picnics in Central Park, which was within walking distance of our apartment. Central Park was where I saw trees and grass. My mother said that the first time she put me down on grass when I was two years old in Queens, I was terrified of it and demanded she pick me up again. We explored Central Park often, and I pretended to fish at the lake there, using a branch with a thread attached and a button tied onto the end.

We walked everywhere, to and from the subway and the bus, and home from Central Park, the library and the grocery store. When we rode the subway, I would grab a newspaper and hold it up close to my face, pretending to read. I talked to my mother loudly as the train rattled down the tracks, regaling her with the facts and other colorful information I had learned in school. People often smiled and rolled their eyes at this kinetic kid who always seemed to be bouncing around.

BLIZZARD

When I was four, a huge blizzard hit New York. There was snow and sleet everywhere. One night I remember my mother and I were crossing a huge avenue filled with traffic going in every direction. When the light turned green, we stepped off the curb and started across. The street was wide. It seemed fully a half a block across from where we stood. Suddenly my mother's heel caught in the trolley tracks and she fell. She struggled to get up but couldn't get her shoe loose. I stood there helplessly, my eyes growing large.

"Mommy, Mommy! The trolley is coming!"

I looked around wildly, needing my mother to get up. Prostrate on the ground and leaning on one elbow my mother batted at me wildly with her free hand. Dark clouds hung in the sky, and the air around us was gray. Dirty snow was piled up along the curb.

"Go! Go, Sandy! Get out of the way!"

"No, Mommy, no!"

The trolley was bearing down on us, its horn blaring, but I wouldn't leave her. I grabbed her arm and pulled and pulled. This did not help at all. Now, my mother couldn't do anything but try to shove me out of the way. Finally, at the last minute, she extricated her shoe from the track, and rolled over just as the trolley screeched to a stop in front of us.

BEAUTIFUL

My mom was beautiful. I boasted to my friends that she was as pretty as the movie star, Betty Grable with her blond hair and blue eyes. I was proud to be with her and called, "Mommy! Mommy!" at the slightest excuse. I wanted everyone to know she was my mother. I thought she was the most beautiful woman in the world. Sailors and young men on the sidewalk often smiled and talked to her as we passed. An outgoing child, I had already decided that we needed a father to complete our family, and asked handsome young men if they wanted to marry my mother. They responded enthusiastically, smiling at her and sometimes palming off a quarter to me. This caused her great embarrassment, but I pocketed the coin. I loved coins and had a collection of them in my doll carriage at home.

These images form an important backdrop of some of my happiest memories in New York City. It was a grimy, gray place compared to the numerous lakes, leafy trees, lawns and pretty houses in Minnesota, but I didn't know that. At night on E.70th Street, part of our evening routine was to wash our ears and neck, and then, with great satisfaction, examine the washcloth for the residue.

IDENTITY

Raised Lutheran, my mother attended St. Paul's Episcopal Church on Fifth Avenue, about six blocks from our house. I sat on the pew next to my mother swinging my small feet back and forth as I looked around. The pageantry of the church service fascinated me. I loved the hymns and the ceremonies of the mass, starting with the entrance of the priest down the aisle with the altar boys following, the raising of the chalice of wine, and the long, sonorous prayers.

Church gave me time to think. I knew there was a god, and while I had no direct or indirect evidence of His existence, I felt it was good to be on the safe side of things and not challenge it. As a practical matter, I didn't debunk Santa Claus, either, since believing in him guaranteed presents at Christmas. I listened to the service, which followed the Book of Common Prayer, much of which is taken from the Bible.

Where was God, anyway? I accepted that He was a mystical, ghostlike figure with white skin, whose face wore a beatific, if equivocal, expression. Privately, I had questions about Jesus, whose countenance was meant to express a peace that "passeth all understanding." I didn't understand why God, who was omnipotent, gave up his only begotten son to save man, and why did Christ allow himself to be used in that way?

Who was I? A little girl, easy to fall beneath God's notice. One part of the Bible particularly preoccupied me: If you sin in your heart, you have already sinned, and think-ing a bad thing is the same as having committed the act. I believed it. I was doomed. Rather than bring this problem to my mother, I swallowed it whole without question and spent my entire childhood believing that I was an inher-ently evil person.

There was further reinforcement of this supposed truth. My mother is white and my father black. Sitting in church among the congregation of white people, with the sun streaming through the stained glass windows, I understood that white was good, and black equated with sin. Darkness is where evil resides. I had dark skin. I must be bad.

I sat on the pew swinging my legs, musing on these things. I knew I was half white and half black. I tried to figure out which part of me was which. As early as four years, I had enough common sense to know a line was not drawn vertically down my center, leaving one side of me white and the other black. The church had taught me that if there is just a little bit of sin, all of me was tainted, was evil. I saw myself as all black.

It didn't dawn on me that there were other ways to look at it. People with black skin could be good and trustworthy, or, from a different perspective, one half of a person could be inside, and the other half his exterior. I knew people could be beautiful on the outside, and not so nice inside. But it hadn't occurred to me to apply this to myself. The whole thing troubled me because it distanced me from my mother, who was unquestionably white, and whom I saw as perfect and whom I desperately did not want to lose.

As exciting as it was to break out on our own and

survive in New York City, my mother was sometimes overcome with the enormity of the task before her— raising a mixed-race child alone, without the support of family. Many times, young, overworked and despondent, my mother sat at the kitchen table after work with her head in her arms, flat-out tired and out of resources. I caught a sense of how bleak she felt and wonder now how she faced it all.

Sometimes we took a subway to a movie theatre where she paid for a ticket and dropped me off.

"You are a very lucky little girl," she said to me. "There is a double feature playing today. You can watch Roy Rogers and Gene Autry. Isn't that wonderful?

"And," she added, "you can watch the movies twice." She admonished, "Don't leave the theatre. I will be back to pick you up at four o'clock." Then she would leave to do some shopping or run errands.

Of course, I didn't stay in my seat and watch the movies the whole time. Soon, I was up and running around, exploring the theatre, climbing up the stairs to the projection booth and looking behind the popcorn counter at the rows of candy and snacks.

When my mother was particularly despondent, I tried to engage her in playing with me. I understood she was sad, in her words, "feeling down." When the prospect of playing with me didn't cheer her up, I tried to counsel her and patiently explained that she needed to get us a home with a father, a dog, a piano and brothers and sisters. This was the solution to all our problems. In my young eyes, ours did not fit the ideal images of family life as depicted in my Dick and Jane reader at school.

At my young age, I had a strong sense of how things should be and sometimes fell into a depression, myself. I would sit in somber thought, perhaps staring out of the window at the activities on the street below, thinking things through, sorting things out. Soon tears would trickle down my face and I would begin to sob disconsolately.

"What's wrong, Sandy?" My mother would gather me on her lap and fold me into her warm arms.

"I just want to be normal," I would cry, distraught, "I'm saaaa-d!"

Where had I gotten the word, "normal"? But I used it. I did not want to be exceptional. I wanted to belong. My mother held me in her lap, rocking me back and forth, perhaps wondering how I could at the same time be happy and excited about life and yet feel so despondent and alone.

Burying my face in the crook of her neck, "I just feel like I'm raining in sunshine."

What I meant was that our family was incomplete, alienated, and out of kilter. We weren't a real family because of the important pieces we were missing.

NEW YORK CITY

PRIVATE SCHOOL

OUR APARTMENT WAS in the Bund section of mid-Manhattan, populated mostly by people who thought Germany should have won the war. When it was time to enroll in kindergarten, my mother was afraid of placing me in the public school on the corner for fear that I would be taunted or bullied. She managed to get a scholarship to cover the tuition of $500 a semester from the Episcopal church to attend its exclusive private school. School was held in its church buildings on Fifth Avenue.

There were four other children in my class. They arrived in chauffeur-driven cars while I walked from our apartment with a little pencil-drawn map in my hand. I was five years old. My mother's employer did not permit her to take off work, so, on the first day, I walked to school by myself. She drew a map on a piece of paper with a pencil and explained how to get to the school from our apartment on E.70th Street.

"Why?" I wailed. I was terrified at the prospect of walking alone to a strange institution called private school. "Why must I go all by myself? What if I get lost?"

My mother reassured me, "You won't get lost, and people will help you. No one would ever hurt a little girl." But I think she was bolstering her own doubts. The danger was very real. I was accosted several times by leery-eyed transients on the watch for someone gullible like me.

One crumpled-up old man leaning against a building used to watch me coming toward him.

"C'mere girlie," holding up a fan of smutty picture cards. "D'ya know what this is, huh?" I didn't understand what I was seeing in the photos, but the lurid tone in his voice was enough to instruct me that the category was unsavory. Taking a look at the cards in his grimy hand, I could tell it was not nice. A grownup would have recognized it as pornography. I learned to skip past these men quickly, run, or even cross the street to avoid them.

"Just ask someone on the corner to help you cross the street," my mother would say. She was implacable, praising me for being a big girl and walking to school all by myself. I bought it. She pointed out how lucky I was to be in such a fine school, where I would study French and have dance lessons, for which I wore special dance slippers, an additional expense from my mother's scant income. Nevertheless, I wanted someone to accompany me and insure my welcome.

I was expected to be on my own a lot. My mother did not tell me that she was shy. She counted on my bubbly and outgoing ways to disarm people into helping me along.

It was a six-block walk from our apartment to the private school on Fifth Avenue— five blocks up 70th Street, turn right and go part way up the block to where a green awning stretched from the gray marble side door of St. Paul's Episcopal Church. The route to private school passed through gradually improving neighborhoods as I walked up from Second Avenue and crossed Lexington, Park, and Madison Avenues, and turned onto Fifth Avenue.

The blocks closest to my apartment were dicey, and I learned to be careful. An old man, what we called a "bum" but who would now be considered a homeless person, sat wedged in a doorway.

"Hey, girlie," he called. "I wanna talk to you." His hand beckoned me to him and tried to grab my wrist as he leered at me, his eyes glittering. I learned to dodge him, too, as I passed his position on the street.

When other kids in my class were dropped off by their drivers who opened their sleek car door in front of the entrance, we smiled at each other and went bobbing into the building.

Walking to school, however, was not scary to me. It was exhilarating. There was so much to see— the cars going back and forth, honking and maneuvering for position as they worked their way through traffic, and the people dressed in all kinds of costumes from all over the world. I stood behind cars on the street and breathed in the sweet, fulsome smell of it their exhaust. I loved the fragrance of the misty, gray cloud of gasses and inhaled them deeply, feeling how lucky I was to be on my own in this exciting city. This may have contributed to my registering a lifetime positive reading on the tuberculosis Mantoux test.

I watched everything as I walked, keeping a careful eye on the sidewalk, "Step on a crack, break your mother's back." Sometimes I got lucky and found a penny or a dime. A couple of times I spotted relatively fresh chewing gum on the sidewalk, scraped it up and popped it into my mouth after first, "Kissing it up to God." I don't remember actually asking grownups to hold my hand as I crossed the street as my mother told me to do. Rather, I looked both ways as I was trained, and then kept close to an adult as he walked across the street.

As I drew closer to Fifth Avenue, I looked forward to passing a pet store that occupied a floor below the street level. I loved the puppies in the window and sometimes actually went down the steps, passing my hand over the wrought-iron railing and peering in at the squirming, helpless animals. A few years later, remembered this experience when I sang, "How much is that doggie in the window? The one with the wag-gily tai-il. How much is that doggie in the window? I do hope that doggie's for sale." [6] I grew up singing all the popular songs of the day.

*   *   *

6 Merrill Bob. 1952, *How Much is That Doggie in the Window*, Sung by Patti Page. Mercury Records, USA and UK.

We had three teachers at private school: a regular teacher, a dance teacher and a French teacher. I was five years old when I entered and was placed in first grade because the school did not have a kindergarten. I learned to read immediately.

Our little class went on field trips. We walked across the George Washington Bridge, took the Staten Island Ferry and visited the Statue of Liberty. Once we went on a walking trip to a fire station, and each of us kids was given the opportunity to jump out of a window into a huge, round safety net below. Some of the kids were too frightened to do it, but I loved jumping from the window and took several turns. The firemen holding the trampoline bounced me high into the air over and over, and I laughed as I flopped on my side and then was sent airborne again.

FIGHTING

"Hah! That's stupid!" I caught a glimpse of him laughing at me, snickering as he turned to his friends. Stanley was a big boy, a lot older than I was. I didn't know him, really, and wasn't even talking to him. He must have overheard my conversation with my best friend, Sofia. We were on E.70th Street, the cars passing in a constant hiss of lurching progress and exhaust fumes. Our block had lots of kids on it, but Sofia and I were the only ones the same age, seven at the time. We were checking the sidewalk as we walked, on the watch for pennies or maybe some chewing gum stuck to the cement. Once I found a dime. It could happen, and in those days you could buy an ice cream cone with a nickel. There was not much to do on the block. We were hanging around waiting to be called in for dinner.

Sofia and I were discussing our favorites: color — blue, favorite movie star—Betty Grable, favorite dessert—

I blurted out, "Yellow berries and black ice cream."

That's when Stanley made fun of me.

"What's wrong with that?" I challenged. My chin jutted out in embarrassment. I hated being ridiculed.

"What's wrong with it?" he sneered. "There ain't no such thing as yellow berries and black ice cream."

I was caught out, exposed and humiliated. This was not the first time my flights of fancy drew skepticism, even derision. I flew at him, pummeling his stomach with my small fists. Stanley fell back a step, caught off guard by my attack. He grabbed me by the shirt and threw me off. The fight was over in a blink. I was up against superior force, and he wouldn't have lowered himself to beating up a little girl anyway.

"Yeah, sure, black ice cream," Stanley sneered as he turned away. He'd already lost interest in me. He took a drag on the stub of cigarette he had snared from the curb and dismissively walked away with his friends.

My mother was a pacifist. I knew the word, all right. It meant no war, not under any circumstances. But my world and hers were ordered on different vectors, and it never occurred to me that pacifism meant I must never get in a physical fight. I fought on the street all the time.

Yellow Berries and Black Ice Cream

All my life I have looked for things that are generally considered impossible and by and large, because I could not separate dreams from reality, many of my dreams have come true. Salmagondi is about searching for my identity. Growing up in New York City and Minnesota before being a mixed-race kid was a concept in the parlance of American culture. In the 1940s I was as much of an anomaly as yellow berries and black ice cream.

Fighting was as common as air; it was a fact of my existence. You defend yourself, or you stick up for others. I never considered I had a choice. What I did have a choice about were my dreams, and that afternoon I thought yellow berries and black ice cream would be an out of this world dessert. What did I know? I was of an age where whimsy and the real world were often fused. I still believe there is nothing wrong in longing for the impossible because some day your dreams may just come true, just as Disney's movie, *Cinderella*, portrays. When my mother took me to see it, I was captivated by the songs and the delightful forest animals in Cinderella's world. I sang the song for months afterward, and it was popular with the other children as well.

> *Have faith in your dreams and someday*
> *Your rainbow will come smiling thru*
> *No matter how your heart is grieving*
> *If you keep on believing*
> *The dream that you wish will come true.*[7]

* * *

I was on my own when I was at school or playing outside on the street. If I needed someone to protect me or tell kids not to tease me, I had to rely on myself.

[7] Woods, Ilene. "A Dream is A Wish Your Heart Makes." Movie, Cinderella. Produced by Walt Disney, 1950.

My mother avoided confrontation. She called it pacifism, a political philosophy I found as removed from day-to-day living as the sentiments put forward in a sermon. Knowing I had no one to stand up for me, I had to be prepared to fight for myself. However, I was bigger than other kids my age, and was willing to fight for what I thought was right.

The protocol for street fighting was draped in codes of honor, if not finer stuff:

First, never hit first: "You start the fight, and I'll finish it," I would promise.

Second, there was the matter of assertions. "You keep that up, and I'll knock your block off!"

"Yeah?" I would say.

"Yeah!" returned my adversary.

"Yeah?" Sneering now, leaning into the other kid's face.

"Yeah!"

The verbal volley would go on for awhile, building tension. During this high-level conversational exchange an audience of children would gather around, cheering as things escalated toward an open fight. My adversary and I would inch closer and closer to each other, sticking our chins out and trying to look mean.

Finally, he (it was invariably a boy) would jab his finger in my chest, and, with resignation, I would take off my glasses, fold them up and hand them to a friend for safekeeping. My adversary would similarly make a show of taking off his jacket, and then we would fight. I usually won because I was bigger and because I had no alternative. I stopped fighting in seventh grade after a boy, whose muscles had begun to harden in adolescence, grabbed me by my sweater and flung me to the floor. I remember skidding down the highly polished hallway. That was my last fight. What we learned on the street was sometimes as important as what we learned in school.

GLASSES

It was my first grade teacher who told my mother I needed glasses. From the time I was four, my mother and Margaret, my nursery teacher from Lenox Hill, and I played pinochle. I couldn't distinguish the queen of clubs from the queen of spades, which was critical because, combined with the jack of diamonds, it made a pinochle.

"Now, see," Margaret explained, "clubs have three rounded circles, and spades look like a spear." As a teacher, she was trained to be patient, but I felt patronized and didn't like it. I squirmed in my seat and sat up straighter, refusing to look at her. I learned never to use that fake, deferential tone when I later became a teacher.

Margaret's attitude dripped with the unspoken

suspicion that I was too dumb to understand. The truth was, I simply couldn't see the detail on the playing cards. I was nearsighted. When my mother got me glasses, my world opened like a flower. I delighted in being able to see people's eyelashes for the first time and could read the letters on street signs. The world opened up for me in even more delightful and colorful ways than it had before. It was just around this time that I started thinking in sentences, rather than in fragmented thoughts.

Still, glasses weren't entirely magical. First there was the teasing. I was called Four Eyes, but since I couldn't see myself from moment to moment and the world was so much clearer with them on, I usually forgot about how I looked with them on. A year later, the light blue, cat-eye glasses with wings my father bought for me when I was living with Mrs. Williams didn't improve my appearance any. My mother had insisted he pay for them. I don't know if he was paying her back by buying frames more suited to an adult than a child, or if he simply didn't know any better.

Because I was tall for my age, my coordination didn't keep up with my growth, and I moved like a little kid in a big kid's body. I was clumsy and broke my glasses several times a year. First it would be a bow that had to be replaced, then the front frame that fit over my nose. Sometimes, I actually broke the lenses. Each time my mother would sigh and say, "Oh, dear, where will we find the money to replace them?" I ran through two or three complete new sets of glasses a year, and as the strength of the prescription changed, I was getting more and more nearsighted.

STRIKE

Despite being the youngest child in my private school class, I was the tallest and the most loquacious. My classmates and I talked happily as we sat at our little table working on our lessons. On one occasion, I thought the teacher answered a classmate dismissively and may have hurt the child's feelings. I told Ms. Scanlon she should apologize. Taken aback, she was not willing to suffer comeuppance from a scruffy, brown charity case. She refused and redirected me to my task. Soon I had fomented a strike; the other children refused to do anything the teacher asked until she apologized. When the priest was called to rein me in, he grabbed me to remove me from the class, and I fought and kicked him. My scholarship was revoked. So, at the age of seven, I had been expelled from school. I was in third grade.

*   *   *

What kind of a kid was I? By all accounts I was lively, noisy, and hyperactive. My mother told me I didn't speak a word until I was almost three, and then I never shut up. I was uncontrollable. Like the mercury from a broken thermometer, adults couldn't pin me under their thumb. I did not intend to be indomitable; it was my response to feeling that I was on my own.

Part of what shaped me was the way we children viewed ourselves in those days: Adults lived in their world, and we lived in ours. We followed their rules because we had to, but we looked for every chance to play and to escape their strictures. I did not play with toys much. Adults were more fascinating to me than dolls, and so I listened to their conversations, thinking my own thoughts about what they were saying. Like Peter Pan, I planned never to grow up. The adult world was fraught with boring responsibilities, while the children's world was one of our own making.

P.S. 33, THE WEST SIDE

Soon I was attending third grade at P.S. 33, on Manhattan's West Side, near where my mother worked. She was a secretary at the Hudson Guild, another settlement house like Lenox Hill. When I entered P.S. 33, lots of things were different. My mom and I took a bus across town. There were 48 kids in my class, most of whom spoke

Spanish. And our teacher, Mrs. Sullivan, devoted most of her effort to teaching English. After chasing down behavior problems, she didn't have much time to teach academics. She spoke no Spanish.

The principal at P.S. 33 was faced with a dilemma. I was reading on a fifth grade level but was only seven years old. Because I had in effect already been "skipped" a grade by not attending kindergarten, I couldn't be skipped again into an academically appropriate grade. I would have to make do in Mrs. Sullivan's class. It was fine with me, however. I was getting another kind of education.

From the time I was young I spent a good part of my day in large buildings— our tenement, childcare centers, Lenox Hill and Hudson Guild, schools, the library, museums and churches. I was on my own a lot and explored these buildings when I had nothing to do. I wandered up and down the back stairs at Lenox Hill and through the other tenements on my street. For some reason I was fascinated with their interior spaces and spent time exploring whenever I got out from under adult supervision. I found back stairways, went up to the roof, and used the elevator, just roaming around, looking. My memories of this do not include other people, each building was an isolated place, and I was a solitary person wandering around in it. A mentor once told me that the reason I read so many mysteries is because my life is a mystery to me, and

I'm trying to figure it out. Freud would say the building, or house, is the self and that it was me in it, a little kid wandering around, exploring it, discovering.

When I went to P.S. 33, I explored nearby buildings after school while I waited for my mother to get off work. Sometimes I was able to get into apartments whose doors were left unlocked. I remember sitting on a pale gray couch looking around at the well-appointed furniture of one apartment and imagining what it was like to live there. On the sidewalk I pretended I was a spy and followed people as they walked, ducking into shadows or standing flat against a building when they turned around to see what I was up to. I was not very subtle, and these evasive moves did nothing to fool the people I was following.

School was fun and exciting. My classmates were children whose fathers were Longshoremen who worked on the docks. Most were Spanish speakers. While their English was limited, their swearing vocabulary was colorful, and I learned to cuss descriptively and with fervor.

Because I spoke English and was good with numbers, when it was time for recess I was put in charge of selling milk and cookies at a little table in the hall outside the classroom. Soon I had pilfered so many shiny nickels and dimes that when my mother cleaned my room one Saturday afternoon, she heard the heavy clink of coins shift in my doll carriage. We had a talk. I had run out of things to buy besides an Almond Joy candy bar and had stashed the coins I stole in the carriage. She was horrified that I had become a thief.

ST PAUL, MINNESOTA

FOSTER HOME

MY MOTHER WAS thrown into a quandary. What should she do? She refused to enroll me in the public school down the block from us, I was no longer welcome at the private school, and P.S 33 wasn't working out. Margaret Williams, my nursery teacher at Lenox Hill, provided a solution. She was a friend of my mother's, well educated, and had taken a special interest in me. After a few expensive phone calls made from a pay phone— we had no telephone in our apartment— Margaret arranged for me to live with her mother in St. Paul. I had already spent a summer with her when I was five, when I attended summer camp at Hallie Q. Brown.

The very first time I flew to Minnesota alone I was five years old. When she bought the ticket my mother lied about my age and said I was seven, the airline's required minimum age for a minor to travel alone. She told me how special I was to fly on an airplane all by myself. If asked, I was to say that I was seven. I was tall enough and outgoing, and I would talk to anyone who would listen. There was one tricky part of the trip that worried me. When we changed planes in Detroit, I was afraid I would not figure out how to get on the next plane. My mother flattered and praised me into believing I could handle it, and I reluctantly accepted the fact that I would somehow have to.

This time it was two years later, and this trip was different. This time I was going to live with Mrs. Williams for the foreseeable future. I pleaded earnestly with my mother, begging her not to send me away. I couldn't imagine living without her. She was the only constant in my chaotic life.

"Please, please, Mommy! Don't send me to live with her. Mommies are supposed to take care of their children. Please, I will be good."

I was beside myself in tears and frustration. It seemed so simple. Why couldn't she understand? I was sitting in her lap, in our apartment on 70th Street, and my mother's arms were around me. My mother was breaking the news in her soft, measured voice. I remember the conversation clearly. I didn't buy it. It seemed there were several times as a child that I felt the need to instruct my mother in the way things should work. I had already tried to get her to remarry.

"I can't, Sandy. You know I want you here with me, but someone has to take care of you while I am at work. You are only seven years old." She refused to be swayed by my tearful entreaties.

Soon I was in St. Paul again, living with a foster mother. Mrs. Williams wasn't a traditional foster parent. She took care of no other children in her home. Nevertheless, she was a stranger to me, a formidable stranger whose home was part of the black community, vastly different from Manhattan's East Side.

I took it all in stride and found ways to have fun. I learned to ride Margaret's 24-inch old, two-wheel bike with fat, red tires, and I made friends with the neighborhood kids. We rolled dry leaves into cigarettes, which we lit and tried to smoke. Because I was on my own so much in New York, I was used to finding my way without the guidance of adults. Of course, I followed adult rules when I had to, but when I ran the streets, nothing of their worldview applied. I operated in the same way in Minnesota— it was a new world to explore.

*   *   *

As you go about your life, you don't take mental notes, you make no value judgments. You just keep going. I didn't realize it, but I must have been lonely. I may have felt abandoned. In the middle of one night, Mrs. Williams found me crying on the narrow stairway going down to her basement from the kitchen. In those days basements didn't have family rooms and weren't fixed up as an extension of the home. They were dark places with a washing machine, a pantry, a furnace and a big pile of coal for heating. In my sleep I must have followed the habits of New York, wandering up and down flights of stairs several times a day. That night I may have been looking for my mother, hoping she could take me home. On several occasions Mrs. Williams found me sobbing on those basement stairs.

"I'm lost. I can't find my mother."

She would put her arms around me, "Come on, baby, let's get you back in bed."

LIVING IN A BLACK COMMUNITY

Mrs. Williams was a dour, strict, no-nonsense African-American woman of some sixty-odd years. She seemed seven feet tall, and towered over me in flower print dresses that buttoned in her ample bosom. Her black shoes that tied and had a raised heel rendered her even taller. She was a god-fearing woman. I don't ever remember Mrs. Williams smiling.

When she laid eyes on me, she must have decided she would get this scruffy child of a permissive Bohemian mother in line. She required that I call her "Ma'am," and polish the staircase and spindles under the bannister for my daily chores. I took a bath once a week on Saturday night. This way, on Sunday mornings, I was ready to go to church properly scrubbed and rectified, smelling like Ivory soap with my three long skinny braids falling away from my face like winter branches.

Mrs. Williams also had me change my underwear

once a week instead of daily. No such disciplines had been imposed on me in New York, where I took a bath every night and changed my underwear every day. When I instructed Mrs. Williams about how we did things in New York, she made it quite clear that we were doing things her way now. In my brazen New York fashion, I tried to set her straight, but Mrs. Williams did not like being challenged, and she shut down the discussion decisively.

Once a month Mrs. Williams washed my hair. This was the beginning of a process familiar in many homes in Black America. After she washed my hair in the upstairs bathroom, she brought me down to the kitchen sat me on a chair, and combed the tangles out.

Chatting with her friends who came over for conversation and coffee, Mrs.Williams placed a can of hair grease on the side of a burner on the gas stove and put a Marcel hot iron in the flame of another. Then she greased my hair and straightened it with the pressing iron, clicking and sliding them down the long locks of my hair. This process is called, "pressing" one's hair.

"Her hair is too fine for that hot comb," one of her friends interjected. Mrs. Green was one of the ladies sitting around the kitchen table, talking and catching up. Mrs. Williams ignored her, and compressed her mouth into a line, as she concentrated on straightening my unruly hair.

"Can you smell it? It's burning," Mrs. Green

pursued. The other ladies looked at me, a pitiable figure, to be sure. But Mrs. Williams was obdurate and ignored them. She was determined to give me the upbringing and discipline my mother had failed to provide.

I heard the ladies' conversation while Mrs. Williams did my hair, not understanding it but getting the gist.

"You know, she just ran wild in New York . . ."

"Mm-HMM, her mother don't know nothin' about bringing up a black child."

Then, Mrs. Williams' voice lowered. Her busy hands stopped clicking the hair comb for a moment and she looked around the group, holding their gaze.

"And her father? Mm! Mm! Mmn! He's running around with blond floozies all UP and down."

Taking up the pressing comb again she directed her eyes significantly at the top of my head, "Poor thing. She don't know WHO she is."

I may as well have been a stuffed toy. Children were meant to be seen and not heard, but I learned a lot from what the adults had to say, even if I didn't understand it.

Mrs. Williams soon accepted the fact that the curling iron burnt my hair, which was too fine for the treatment and broke off. I learned that not only was I not white enough to be accepted by white people in New York, but I was inadequate as a black person in St. Paul. My hair could not withstand the beautification ritual that took place in kitchens of black homes all over America. It wasn't strong enough. Mrs. Williams had to content herself with brushing it furiously.

"Hold yoh haid! Hold yoh haid!"

I quickly learned not to cry and to gauge just how much to tug my head in opposition to her vigorous brush strokes so my head would not snap back with each one. I came away from these sessions with pitifully thin, oily braids, one on the side of my forehead and two down my back.

*　　*　　*

Mrs. Williams took exception to my looking her in the eye and speaking clearly in my New York accent.

"Don't mark me," she accused repeatedly. I finally realized she meant, "mock." My New York diction was different, nondeferential and direct and it offended her.

When Mrs. Williams called me from the porch steps to come in for dinner, I yelled, "Whaaa?" from the other end of the street. This was what we did in New York. My mother would lean out the window on the fifth floor and call, and I yelled back from wherever I was on the block. Mrs. Williams took my response as an act of extreme disrespect and demanded that when she called I come immediately, stand in front of her with my hands at my sides and say, "Yes, Mrs. Williams?" She often reminded me to call her, Ma'am. There were a lot of adjustments to my childrearing in St. Paul, and for the most part, I was the better for it.

ST. PETER CLAVER SCHOOL

I was enrolled in third grade at St. Peter Claver Catholic School, which was a few blocks from our house at 922 St. Anthony Avenue. Most of the students were black, as were the nuns, who were very strict. My time at that school wasn't to last long. Culturally, I had a lot to adjust to. Coming from a city far away, the other kids found my standup manner bold and exciting. My New York accent delivered brash, up front, loud language. Uncouth by Midwestern standards, I didn't adapt well to the rigorous classroom discipline of the nuns, which was quite different from the wild Spanish cacophony and Mrs. Sullivan's yelling in my third grade classroom at P.S. 33.

I had a bad habit of shouting out because I was so eager to give the right answer, and I was so excited to tell the nun first, I had trouble sitting calmly and waiting to be called on. One day, Sister Theresa walked up the aisle toward me. Her lips were pressed into a thin line, and she forcefully slapped a yardstick against the palm of her hand. She had had enough of my calling out and my further antics, designed to make the other kids in the room laugh. Still, the smartest and tallest child in the class, I was afraid of no one. I stared at her boldly as she marched up to me.

"Stand up, Sandy."

I stood, holding Sister Theresa's eyes, refusing to bow to her will or to apologize, a response which might have gotten me off the hook. She struck my legs with the yardstick several times. I bit my lip and blinked back tears, standing even taller against the pain. When she was finished, she swirled around in her black habit and sailed majestically to the front of the class. I looked down at my legs and, alarmed at the large, red welts her punishment had left, cursed her in words she may not have been used to hearing. I was outraged. I had never even been spanked before. Tears of anger and insult streaming down my face, I shouted at her and threatened that my mother would sue her. I was shipped back to New York.

That summer I went to camp in upstate New York. In the fall, my mother sent me back to live with Mrs. Williams, and talked St. Peter Claver into accepting me again, this time in Sister Marguerita's fourth grade class. She was, they assured my mother, a no-nonsense disciplinarian who would keep me in line.

ST PAUL, MINNESOTA

COMO LAKE

MY FATHER'S ROOMING house was a short distance from where I lived with Mrs. Williams, so he was able to visit me occasionally during my time in Minnesota. On one occasion he picked me up to go to the movies. He drove up in a car filled with friends. The car pulled up to the curb, and they all got out to say hello to Mrs. Williams. She was holding my hand as we stood outside her house on St. Anthony Avenue. I was eight years old.

From my short height I saw a flurry of nylon-stockinged knees and ankles, red lipstick and smiling faces as his friends laughed and jostled to make room for me. A leggy blonde Mrs. Williams later called a floozy scooted over to the center of the front seat and invited me in. The smoke from the cigarette in her right hand made shivery circles in front of my face as I slid in beside her. The mood of carefree joy was infectious, and I was happy to be with these loud, colorful grownups.

We went to see the movie, *Laura*, which was a slow-moving, moody, crime drama about a man who lost a beautiful blonde woman he loved. I was too young to catch the details of the plot— the man who loved Laura was a detective, and she was murdered— but I did catch the dark mood of desolation, which still affects me today when I hear the musical theme of this film noir. I didn't recognize it explicitly, but the movie mirrored my father's feelings for my mother who was still in New York. When we emerged from the theater it was dark outside, and I felt sad and alone.

I was actually glad to get back to Mrs. Williams' house that night, unusual, because normally, there was nothing I wanted more fervently than to escape her care and return to New York. She had saved dinner for me. Mrs. Williams must have caught something of my mood, because I was unusually subdued. It had been a long day, and I was dreaming before my head hit the pillow that night, but I heard her murmur, "Good night, baby," as she kissed my forehead and tucked me in.

*   *   *

The following spring, in April, my mother suddenly came to St. Paul. I didn't know why, but Mrs. Williams made it clear that I would not be going back to New York with her when she left. My disappointment was lost in my joy that I was going to see my mommy! She and Mrs. Williams talked for a long time in the living room with me fidgeting around, not really listening, my eyes on my mother's face. I was fascinated by the miracle of her arrival. She was so beautiful! I could barely contain myself.

My mother had driven her old, black 1943 Buick

out to St. Paul. She turned to me with a smile, "How would you like to go to Como Lake?"

I was beside myself. Como Lake was one of nineteen lakes in the St. Paul-Minneapolis area. Everyone in our neighborhood either went to Lake Phalen, which was better for swimming, or Como Lake, which was bigger and more beautiful. Minnesota is known as *The Land of Ten Thousand Lakes*.

We clambered into her car and drove to my father's rooming house and picked him up. Then we all drove out to Como Lake. There was an awkward tension in the car as we drove, an air of forced civility. My mother asked my father how he was doing, and he replied stiffly, something brief. His conversational forays were met with equal awkwardness. It was ironic, because I had long held a dream that my mother and father and I would live together in our own home and that we would be a whole family. This did not feel like family. On the few occasions I had visited him, I found my father to be gruff. He did not seem to know what to do with me. He was a mystery to me, and I had a suspicion he might be dangerous. I sat behind my parents in the back seat watching them exchange polite small talk as my mother drove. I looked out the window, thinking.

When we got to the park, we walked around aimlessly. My father wore a dark suit and a fedora, and my mother's gray coat covered a silk dress. She wore heels and nylon stockings and was looking very pretty. Mrs. Williams had dressed me up in my Easter Sunday dress and patent leather shoes.

They encouraged me to go play, but I was uneasy about ruining the sheen of my shoes by going too close to the lake and stepping in mud. I did not run around or climb trees, but instead wandered within earshot of their words, which sounded flat and emotionless and oddly echoed one another, my mother's soft, feminine voice and my father's low, steady rumble. We walked near the Lakeside Pavilion, and I was reminded of the mood in the movie *Laura*, that I had seen with my father. This, coupled with the weird tension between them, made me watchful and sad.

Then my father turned in my direction. "Come here!" he called. I looked at them standing together and trotted over. He pulled me to him and placed his hands on my shoulders, pressing down as we both faced my mother.

It was some kind of standoff.

"Don't leave me." He was staring at my mother. The timbre of his voice had gone funny. It sounded weak, which I didn't like. *Was he sad?* He sounded defeated.

"I can't," she said.

I didn't understand what my mother was talking about. *Can't what? What happened?*

"Tell her!" My father shook my shoulders.

He was talking to me. I craned my neck up to look into his face. *What was he talking about?* I saw my mother's eyes widen. Too much was going on that I didn't understand. For once in my hyperkinetic life I remained mute.

"Tell her you want us to be a family." He looked at her again.

"Please!" he begged, his eyes locked on hers. We were trapped in an uncomfortable tableau, surrounded by blue sky, brown tree trunks, the forest green of grass and the green boughs of trees. None of us wanted to be there.

My mother demurred softly as my father pled with her.

I don't know how we got home. That is the end of that memory. Eight months later Mrs. Williams packed my clothes in my brown cardboard suitcase, gave me a bath and washed my hair. She put plenty of grease on it and braided it into three long, skinny braids, one at the side of my forehead, and the other two running down my back. She dressed me in my Sunday dress, the navy blue coat with white lace under the collar my mother had sewn for me, and my black patent leather shoes. Then she drove me to the airport in Minneapolis.

"You're going to live with your mother and new father," she explained as she drove. She walked me down the aisle of the plane to my seat. Then she kissed me and hugged me tight, turned around and got off the plane. I was a seasoned traveler by then and stared out the window on that bright, sunny day, impatient for the plane to take off.

My mother divorced my father and remarried in October, 1952. She had stopped in St. Paul to let my father know that she was divorcing him. She worked in Reno as a maid for six months to gain residency for her divorce. A whole new life awaited me in New York City.

LITTLE BO TEET

That summer Mrs. Williams sent me to the day camp sponsored by Hallie Q. Brown, the same settlement house where my mother and father had worked during that glorious, politically active time when they were in college and fell in love. I had no idea of the historic connection, nor that in ten years I would have two sisters who would also enjoy its summers while I worked there as a counselor.

One of the kids at camp was Little Bo Teet. Bo, short for brother, was Roscoe Joe's little brother, hence the nickname. He was built like a link sausage, muscular and solid as a bull. He was a shade shorter than I, but what he lacked in height he made up for in weight. Teet was always laughing at people, kind of snuffling into the back of his hand, eyes on you and running away at the same time. He was a bully.

His brother, Roscoe Teet was a dope fiend. He started enjoying the pleasures of codeine in Cheracol cough syrup when he was about thirteen. He boldly tipped the bottle of dark purple liquid up and drank surreptitiously in the weak yellow incandescent light of a doorway at parties. In high school Roscoe moved on to heroin. He became a drug dealer and held the respect of a tribal lord and some of the mystery of a shaman. Roscoe was tall and skinny, the bones under his skin kind of rumpled up like sticks under a blanket. He was of a dark, dark complexion, light only catching reflection in the creases of his cheeks. By contrast, Little Bo had rich buttery, brown skin, and he would have resembled a Campbell's Soup kid, if the company had diversified their advertising in those days.

Roscoe had contracted polio when he was young and limped on one withered leg. He managed to turn that limp into a black man's swagger— slow, dip, and easy— and because he was deformed, he was scary. He never smiled when he looked at you. Teet was scared of Roscoe, too, but he still took advantage of his mystique. When Teet took things too far and needed refuge, he found protection in Roscoe's shadow. Teet was always laughing with a malicious humor, but Roscoe never laughed. They were opposite corners in the broken structure of a collapsed family unable to cope with Roscoe's early childhood disease. These are things, like air, that I understood without saying. Because we were poor, there was always an underlying dark side to our lives, which is probably why we lost ourselves in total joy whenever we got the opportunity.

*   *   *

We're on the upward— trail!
We're on the upward trail!
Singing, singing, everybody's singing
As we go![8]

I loved that camp song. The older boys and male counselors grouped at the back of the bus sang loudly as the bus drove us to the lake. Their big bass voices, repeated each line with vigorous gusto. I felt I was part of a huge army of kids as we flew down the highway.

We also sang,

Do Lord, oh do Lord, do remember me.

Really belting out the line,

He looked a-waay, be-yo-ond the blue! [9]

And the basso voices in the back would echo low,

"HO-RI-ZON."

There were no seat belts, no adults nagging us to stay seated, just songs, laughter, and calling back and forth

---

[8] Kirkham, Oscar (1880-1958). We're on the Upward Trail. Camp song of Church of Latter Day Saints.

to one another.

> *99 bottles of beer on the wall, 99 bottles of beer.*
> *If one of the bottles should happen to fall,*
> *there would be 98 bottles of beer on the wall.*[10]

By the time we got to Carver Lake, we were a troop of happy kids looking forward to having Fun in the Sun, the slogan of Hallie Q. Brown Summer Camp. Our day was filled with fun activities, running games, swimming, crafts and songs.

We each brought our lunch in a brown paper bag. Mrs. Williams made me two bologna sandwiches on white bread with a chopped pickle sandwich spread. No lettuce. There was an apple. No cookies, no chips. The camp provided milk. A good eater, I always consumed my entire lunch. We ate out on the grass in front of the lake, sitting in small groups by trees or in the open spaces.

One day I sat with my friend, Wanda, and some other kids, talking and carefully putting our waxed paper back in the bags when we were through.

Bo Teet came trotting by, his lopsided grin sliding across his face. He stooped and grabbed Wanda's lunch bag with her sandwich inside and ran away, a familiar game amongst us kids.

[9] Public Domain. Do Lord. Spiritual.
[10] Public Domain. Mid-20th Century. 99 Bottles of Beer on the Wall. Camp Song.

"I got it! I got it!" he called, inviting Wanda to chase him.

Wanda scrambled up, her little feet flying as she raced after him, but Teet was faster than she was. He enjoyed the game and laughed like a hyena, circling our spot and slowing just enough so that she almost caught up. Maybe he was tiring of the game, unexpectedly, Teet threw her lunch bag into the lake. Wanda, out of breath, slowed to a halt. Her face crumpled in disbelief and tears sprang to her eyes, all to Teet's great delight. The bag was lying in the water's edge, but her lunch was soggy and ruined as she picked it up.

I felt Wanda's humiliation and helplessness. Outrage bloomed in my chest. It is one thing to tease and play, but why did he have to do that? I rose to my feet, my chin jutted out, and I ran after him. Teet loved this. The game would continue. I chased and chased after him as he ran in looping spirals, Teet looking over his shoulder at me. After awhile, he tired and ran more slowly. I came on him like a locomotive.

The truth was, I didn't know how to fight or how to best land a punch, but I was taller than he was and had a longer reach. And I was angry. I shoved him on the back, grabbed him by the shoulders and pushed him. Out of breath, Teet stumbled and fell. I jumped on top of him, straddling him with my knees, and punched him in his face and on his chest.

Gradually, the fight went out of him. It wasn't a fair fight any more. I had won. But I kept on hitting Bo. I got to my feet, out of breath, and kicked him in the back and then the stomach as he rolled over and over in the grass. He cried, his arms protecting his face and head. A switch had turned on inside me. I couldn't stop beating up Little Bo Teet.

A dim awareness told me there was no point, no more fight left in the boy, and I felt sick to my stomach. I wanted to throw up. I had never been in a fight that I had won so decisively. Usually, both sides got a bruise or a bloody cut and the fight ended by unspoken agreement, even though neither party would have admitted it. I knew in that hot afternoon sun that I held a pent-up rage that existed independent of the injustices I so proudly fought for. I turned away, confused and disgusted with myself, filled with none of the happy pride I usually carried away from a fight.

* * *

That September, I went back to St. Peter Claver, and entered fifth grade. It was to be only for a short time, but I didn't know that. I entered the classroom laughing and calling out to my friends. Some of us had walked to school together, and we were looking around for a desk to sit in, eager to compare our binders and school supplies newly purchased for the start of the school year. I breezed through the doorway, happy to be back in school with friends, when my progress was checked by the strong grip of a hand on my arm.

Sister Celestine had stopped me and looked down, through her sparkling, rimless glasses, into my eyes. The soft, creamy beige of her face was dotted with freckles, and I looked up at her, noting the tight white fabric of the habit that framed her face.

"I don't want to have anything to do with you," she enunciated in a low, determined, voice. "I know who you are, and you're not going to get away with anything."

Apparently the school had had enough of my antics, and I was on the short string of probation.

"Yeah. Okay," I responded and shrugged my arm out of her grip. I was bemused, not insulted, and looked forward to having fun in school. I was unaware of my reputation as a hard-to-manage, pain-in-the-neck kid, and hadn't connected Sister Celestine's edict to Mrs. Williams' warning before I set off for school that morning.

"Now, you be good in school, all right? Do what the teacher say."

NEW YORK CITY

THE BRONX

WHILE I WAS IN MINNESOTA, my mother met and fell in love with the son of Russian Jews. His parents had escaped the pogroms in Kiev, Ukraine and they immigrated to the Bronx. My mother met Jack Pineles at a folkdance party at the Henry Street Settlement House in Manhattan. Actually, she was on a double date with Margaret Williams, and Jack was Margaret's date. But Jack took one look at my mother and his heart was hers. This caused a rift between Margaret and my mother that took years to heal.

My mother moved to Reno while I was still in St. Paul, and worked there as a maid for six months while she gained residency. When her divorce was final, she and Jack got married in Reno. They drove to Concord, California to visit my Aunt June and Uncle Hank. My Grandfather Porter now lived with them. In my mother's biography she said she didn't fly me out for the celebration because she didn't want to subject me to the disapproval of her father. Jack and my mother then moved to the apartment where he and sister, Carol, lived in the Bronx.

I remember when they sent for me. It was Thanksgiving, and I flew from St. Paul to LaGuardia Airport by myself. Of course, by this time I was an old hand at flying, but I was really excited about this trip. First of all, I would live with my mother again, but second, I would have a father! We would be a real family. The plane landed on a sunny, cold day, and I was wearing my Sunday dress and navy blue coat my mother had sewn for me. My hair was carefully brushed, oiled and braided, and the tops of my white socks were neatly turned down to meet the tops of my black, patent leather shoes.

In those days there was no jet-bridge to connect a plane to a walkway. Passengers descended stairs to the tarmac and then walked into the terminal. My mother and Jack were waiting at the foot of the steps. Coming down, I was so busy taking it all in, that I didn't see them. I had observed the buildings of New York City as we landed and was remembering how much I loved this urban place that I was so proud to hail from. As soon as my foot hit the tarmac I was bowled over by my mother, who swooped down and wrapped me in her arms.

"Sandy! Sandy!" She was laughing and crying, burying me in her warm coat. She had dropped to her knees, and I looked directly into her eyes. I could smell her lipstick as she planted kisses all over my face. Gradually, I caught a glimpse of gray twill slacks standing behind her as she let me go. I pushed my glasses up on my nose with one finger and looked at my mother and my new father.

Jack was of medium height with a big belly. He weighed about 190 pounds and the wisps of curling blond hair on his high, receding forehead riffled in the wind. I immediately approved. He was perfect! Finally, I had a father. I had a family.

We caught a taxi and drove to their apartment. Sitting between them in the back seat, I looked up at their faces and placed their hands on top of each other in my lap. They laughed happily at this acknowledgement of their union.

*   *   *

We lived in a two-and-a-half-room apartment with its own bathroom on the fifth floor at 3470 Cannon Place in the Bronx, not too far from Van Cortland Park. They were called the Shalom Aleichem Apartments, which I pronounced *Shula Malechem* because that was how I heard it pronounced. The irregularly-shaped block was filled with buildings along Cannon Place, which curved and ran into Giles Place. Our mail was delivered to our mailbox in the foyer, regardless of the street written on the envelope.

My mother and Jack slept in the bedroom, off of which was the bathroom. Jack's sister, Carol, and I slept in the living room. Carol was about seven years older than I was. She had my mother's rollaway bed, the studio couch, and I slept on a dilapidated brown velvet, three-cushion sofa. My mother put me to sleep in their bed at night, and then Jack carried me to the living room sofa when they were ready to go to bed. There was a tiny galley kitchen, which barely had enough room for all of us to sit and eat at one time.

Jack and his sister, Carol, had grown up in this apartment complex. It was where their mother and father had lived when they came to New York. Jack's father died when he was young, and his mother passed away when he was 19 and Carol was 15. Youth and Family Services did not check on them. Carol stayed in high school, and Jack got a job and took care of them both.

Achieving excellent grades all through high school, Jack went to CCNY, City College of New York, at night. It took him nine years to earn his bachelors in chemistry. When he met my mother he was working at Standard Brands as a lab chemist.

Jack was seven years younger than my mother. When they married, he was 27, and still a kid in many ways. Sometimes, when we drove from the Bronx to Manhattan, Jack sat in the back seat with me while my mother took the steering wheel. Jack was handsome, and I loved his cocky masculinity.

Jack didn't have a driver's license, so my mother did all the driving. Traffic was always a nightmare, and we found ourselves sitting in a gridlock of cars from both directions. Sometimes Jack gave me a water gun, and pulled one out for himself. From the back seat, we played gangster, rolled down the windows and ducked down as if taking cover. On a cue, we popped up, guns blazing and sprayed water at the drivers on either side of us. After a hit we immediately ducked down again, out of sight, leaving my mother to receive the outraged diatribes in response. My mother, embarrassed, gripped the wheel with both hands and looked straight ahead.

Each of us, my mother, Jack, and I, was starved for family. We appreciated belonging to each other and spent many joyful times together. Jack was completely in love with my mother. He said she looked like the Swedish actress Ingrid Bergman.

Jack and I, united in our ardor for my mother, immediately became fast friends and allies. He encouraged me to work hard in school, to question the teacher, and to be a smart aleck.

If someone picked on me, he told me to finish the fight only if the other guy started it. Jack regaled me with stories of fights between the Italians and the Jews when he was growing up.

"My first fight ended quickly," he recounted. "He punched me in the nose, and that was it!"

Jack wasn't ashamed of having been beaten up, and he didn't care if I won a fight. He wanted me to stand up for myself and let the results be what they would be.

Jack's language was filled with Yiddish expressions,

and he liked to crack jokes and play word games. He called me Louie Goniff and Blue Tooth Louie and made up puns all the time. When I complained that it was hard to sweep the floor, he would yell, "Use yer head!" He was irreverent and said things like, "Horse shit!" I loved him.

Filling my list of components for a complete family was off to a good start. Wasting no time, I reminded my parents that I needed a dog, brothers and sisters, and a piano.

Jack still worked at Standard Brands as a chemist, and my mother was still working at the Hudson Guild Settlement House on the West Side. Once again, there was a period of three hours when I was on my own after school. I would climb the five flights of steps to our apartment— this time I had a key— and scramble two eggs with butter in a small iron skillet on the stove in our tiny kitchen. I made a sandwich using the unique, small rectangular slices of whole wheat Masterbread and ate it at the table with a glass of milk. Fortified, I then went outside to play for a few hours.

My mother said we ate a lot of spaghetti in those days, but sometimes she asked me to help prepare dinner by putting on potatoes so that they would be ready when she got home. I responded positively, I would be coming in at about that time, anyway. But, when faced with the task for the first time, I realized I didn't know how to tell when the potatoes were done. Using the house phone, I dialed 411, Information.

"How can you tell when potatoes are boiled?" I asked. The operator was vexed and suspected I was teasing her, but she must have sensed the worry in my voice and finally told me to stick a fork in them, and if they were soft, the potatoes were cooked.

Although both my sisters are excellent cooks, I don't remember my mother teaching me how to bake a cake, make cookies, or follow a recipe. To be fair, that might have been due to a lack of receptivity on my part. Later, when I did cook, I hated following recipes, reasoning that if you did so, all you would get is exactly what was expected. I thought of cooking as a creative process and liked to deviate from the recipe, adding as many different ingredients as I could. For me, cooking was more like playing at chemistry than homemaking.

My parents were worried that I was on my own for long periods of time after school, and got me a mutt from the dog pound. I named him Goldie, but Jack insisted on calling him Pooch, which outraged me because it was my dog. However, I was on the losing end of the argument. Pooch avoided me like the plague, baring his teeth and growling murderously when I tried to cuddle or play with him. I was too rambunctiously affectionate for Pooch's liking, and he quickly learned to respond to my parents and the name, Pooch, when they called.

Every day after school I took Pooch out for a walk. Locked in the house since early morning, he couldn't hold his piss when I unlocked the door and he pissed on me in delight as he leapt up and down. I could barely attach his leash to the collar of this furry froth of fur.

In the spring, Jack and I walked Pooch across a vacant lot filled with weeds. A short while later I walked Pooch the same route after school. I noticed the weeds had tiny, white blossoms on them and thought how pleased my mother would be if I brought home a bouquet of flowers for her. I ripped up an armful by the root. The flowers were still beautiful, even with the stringy roots attached.

When I came home, I greeted my mother with my arms full of poison ivy blossoms surrounding my face, and proud to show my love to her, gave the bouquet to my mother.

"Oh, Sandy! How beautiful, but . . . aren't they poison ivy?"

I came down with a horrible case of poison ivy. My eyes were swollen shut, and my mother took me to the doctor. She and Jack still put me to sleep in their bed, and after a few days of Jack carrying me to the couch for the night, he contracted poison ivy all over his chest. He laughed about it and said there was nothing he would not do for his daughter.

*   *   *

Jack really loved me. "Would you like me to adopt you?" he asked. "You would have my last name, and I would be your father."

I thought about it. "No, that's all right. I already have a father."

I don't think I realized what Jack was offering. I just felt that some things were immutable. I already had a father— there was no way of changing that and all it brought with it. Adopting me wouldn't change it.

"I'll just be Sandy Rogers, that's who I am."
We talked a little more. "Do you want to call me Daddy, anyway?"

"No, you aren't my father," I said thoughtfully. "I'd have to use a different name. You seem more like a Pop," and I laughed a little, thinking of his big round belly. I ended up calling my stepfather, Jack from then on. After all, that was his name.

I was unaware of what Jack was offering me. He wanted to demonstrate his love for me and make me his legal daughter as part of a legitimate family. However, I had considered it the height of farce to change my name to Sandra Pineles. I had no idea what I was going to deal with as my life rolled forward, but I wanted to face it as myself.

155

P.S. 95

After Thanksgiving, my mother enrolled me in fifth grade at P.S. 95 in the Bronx. I was the only black kid in an enrollment of mostly Jewish students. Being the kid who was different, who hadn't enjoyed friendships with the same group of friends since kindergarten, was not a new experience for me. I had spent my childhood looking in from outside. I didn't belong, didn't fit in. I didn't mind, though. I never knew any different, and the trade-off was the exposure to many kinds of people and cultures. Life was exciting and fun for me, but all the abrupt transitions might explain my deep need to belong to a family.

New York City imposed an indelible sense of identity on me. I felt as if I was part of the most important, most alive city in the world. I was not an insignificant speck lost in a big city, I was one of its constituent parts. I didn't live in a tiny apartment on the top floor of a tenement, I lived in New York!

*　　*　　*

Building structures were packed into my sense of self. It may have been the P.S. 95 building that was at the center of another of my recurring dreams. In the dream I was late to school. My classroom was on the third floor. The huge, red brick building filled a square block and was four stories high. In the dream I rushed into the building after the bell had rung and all the kids were in class.

The halls were silent and empty. I was desperate to get to my classroom quickly. I was faced with a dilemma: Take the stairs or the elevator? The stairs were slower, but the elevator, which was discouraged, was faster. The problem was, it was a dangerous contraption.

The elevator was unpredictable. Sometimes it did not stop at the right floor. Instead, it shot straight up and out through the roof, jolting me breathlessly awake from my nightmare. It was terrifying. The elevator could also hurtle horizontally or vertically right through the building. On the occasions it flew sideways, it passed through the other rooms on the floor and on into space, I could see the wooden framing of the walls whiz by, each room possibly representing a different day or period in time.

I figured out years later that the symbolism of the dream was the elevator car represented my self traveling out of control, laterally through space or up through time. I think it represented my fear of what was to come and of life getting out of control. While I was a happy-go-lucky kid always looking for fun or trouble— sometimes they were the same— on some level my psyche must have been scrambling to keep up with the riotous changes in my life.

*   *   *

A SHULA MALECHEM CHRISTMAS

Even though we lived in a Jewish community, my mother insisted on celebrating our first Christmas together as a family. We got a tree and decorated it, and it was beautiful. Twelfth Night, January 6th, also Jack's birthday, came and went. We kept that tree up for months after Christmas passed, its soft colored lights warming our living room in the evening. My parents had grown uneasy about how to get rid of it because of what the neighbors might think, so we ended up keeping it. The tree completely dried out and shed needles every time it was touched. Finally, after Easter, Jack hauled the tree out the living room window and dropped it over the side of the fire escape to my mother, who was waiting below. They hauled it to a vacant lot. They were worried that the neighbors would criticize Jack and Carol for celebrating Christmas.

*   *   *

In the spring of that year, 1953, I turned ten years old. My hair had grown quite long. My mother had always had a difficult time brushing and combing my wild, tangled hair. Finally, she had had enough and cut it all off into a "poodle" cut, which she declared was fashionable at the time, very short curls, maybe two inches long. There was no more trouble combing my hair anymore. After I washed it, I let it go its own way. I was to keep my hair short for the next twenty years.

*   *   *

Built side by side, the Shula Malechem apartments ringed an oblong city block and were connected by underground tunnels, which we called, "the catacooms," catacombs. When my friends and I played too loudly or broke something, the super chased us, yelling that he was going to have our parents punish us. We raced up the stairs to the roof, hopped over the ledge to another building, clattered down the stairs to the catacombs in the basement, and came up again in another building, invariably escaping the winded, frustrated property manager.

I remember one time we were on the roof talking, spoofing around, and dropped bricks over the side to the sidewalk to watch them fall. Today I shudder to think what would have happened if we had hit a passerby.

One night after we had all gone to bed, I overheard my mother say to Jack in their bedroom.

"We have to get out of New York. Sandy is turning into a juvenile delinquent."

On one of the hottest days in September, they packed up my mother's 1943 Buick with all our pots and

Ralph Jumps, the Bronx,
photo by Stephen Shames, www.stephenshames.com

pans, bedding, clothes, and our dog, Pooch, and we set out to drive to St. Paul, Minnesota. Carol stayed in New York.

My mother was the only driver because the State of New York had pulled Jack's license for hot-rodding. She was pregnant, with my sister, Nancy, and so big that she had trouble getting behind the steering wheel.

The trip took three days. We stopped and paid for a room each night in people's homes along the way. We had packed in such a hurry that at one point our pressure cooker fell out onto the Pennsylvania Turnpike, causing a ruckus on the roadway. My mother pulled the car and trailer over, and Jack rescued the valuable cooking pot.

TWIN CITIES, MINNESOTA

THE MOVE TO MINNESOTA

MY MOTHER MADE the decision to move our family to Minnesota, and Jack simply agreed. He never argued about it. Never having lived anywhere but New York, this was another demonstration of his loyalty to our family. But Jack spent the rest of his life complaining that there wasn't a decent delicatessen outside New York, and you couldn't find an authentic Jewish bagel in the Twin Cities, much less an egg crème. A beverage unique to New York, egg crèmes are made in a tall glass with milk, soda and chocolate syrup. My sisters and I weren't allowed to drink soda, hot dogs, or junk food, but Jack did. He made egg crèmes for himself and drank them while sitting at the end of the dining room table and reading the New York Times. He loved chocolate covered cherries, and had a sweet tooth, which he passed on to my sisters.

At first we lived in a rural suburb of the Twin Cities. We rented a little cottage on Turtle Lake, and I entered fifth grade at Snail Lake School. The place was meant for summer vacations and was not insulated. We couldn't keep it warm as the days grew shorter and colder with the coming winter. We had to wear our jackets indoors. The cottage was set on a large, beautiful property with shady trees and grass leading all the way down to the lake and was set back from the water about 200 feet. Surrounded by trees, it was like a fairy tale home out of one of my books. Essentially a city kid, I climbed one of the trees and got stuck up there. Jack came and helped me down. My parents bought me white, lace-up ice skates, and I learned to skate on Turtle Lake that winter.

A rural school bus took me to school. I remember the kids throwing rocks at me and calling me, "nigger." I knew they meant to be hurtful, but I was bemused by the term. It meant nothing to me. In school, I had established myself as the smartest in the class. A city kid, I was more articulate than the other students and could cuss impressively. I was used to being on my own and thought I knew how to handle myself.

DINKY TOWN

Within a few months Jack got a job as a chemist in the University of Minnesota Hospital lab, and we moved to the first floor of an old house in Minneapolis, five blocks from the entrance to the campus. The neighborhood was called Dinky Town, and is the geographic equivalent the Telegraph Avenue area around the UC Berkeley campus today. Both 15th Avenue SE in Minneapolis and Telegraph Avenue in Berkeley dead-end into a street that runs past the entrance to the university campus. Much later, when I moved to California, I confused the two in my dream imagery.

I attended Marcy School about five blocks from our house. My mother was hugely pregnant, just about to deliver my sister. Nancy was born on December 15, 1953.

A great big city bus hissed to a stop at our corner every 25 minutes, dropping off and picking up passengers. Then, with a mighty wheeze, it chugged on again. The noise and fumes were not bothersome to me. I was used to New York traffic and found the racket reassuring in what was a comparatively quiet city.

We lived at 917 – 15th Avenue SE. A block and a half behind our house was an open field filled with weeds and debris. Through it ran railroad tracks where I heard the lonely whine of freight trains rolling through at night. It was in that field that I saw my first solar eclipse and noticed the unending horizon in every direction. It was unfamiliar after living with a sky criss-crossed with the corridors of buildings in New York. Our backyard was a small, disreputable patch, mostly consumed by a decrepit one-car garage. An alley ran behind our house

We lived in an old Victorian that had been converted into a duplex for rental. The front room with bay windows facing the street was my parents' bedroom. Two large French doors opened from it into the living room, which, despite its inset window seats, was dark because of the houses standing close by on either side of us. The houses on 15th Avenue SE were built close together so that as many people as possible had access to public transportation to go to work. My small room was dark and opened off the hall that led from the front door to the living room, and the kitchen and bathroom filled out the width at the back of the house. The kitchen was small, which was normal for us. Our kitchen in New York had been too small for all of us to sit in comfortably. We didn't see a problem having supper at a table close enough to the sink and the stove to touch them.

I walked to a used bookstore a few blocks from our house and bought books for 25 cents with my weekly allowance. I read *Great Expectations* by Dickens, *Little Women, Jo's Boys, Rebecca of Sunnybrook Farm* by Louisa May Alcott, and *Understood Betsy* by Dorothy Canfield Fisher. It was a treat to buy books with my own money, and I enjoyed going up and down the aisles of the small, crowded, corner bookstore looking for treasures.

CHORES

Ever since I was a kid I have hated chores, and because there was no way around them, I created inventive work-saving techniques to get through them more quickly. When we arrived in Minnesota, my mother really needed to do some housework, but I was such a crazy ten-year old that I wasn't much help. I hadn't caught on to the utility of keeping things clean and orderly. It must have vexed my mother's patient, pacific heart to have to explain over and over that house work must be done.

She would sigh and say, "Cleaning house is virtuous and makes one feel clean and good," hoping I would long for the same saintly salvation. I could tell she believed what she was saying, but it was the kind of conversation that made me realize my mother and I had very different world views.

One of my chores was to wash and dry the dishes after dinner. I hated it. There were so many steps to washing dishes, it seemed I would never get to go outside to play. First, I had to gather the dirty dishes from the kitchen table and fill the shallow sink with water and detergent. Then I washed the dishes, rinsed them and placed them in the rack. As if that weren't enough, I also had to dry the dishes and put them away so that I could wash the pots and pans.

Cooking was a messy task. It required the scrubbing of pots and pans with Brillo pads and guaranteed lots of yucky scraps all over the place. As often as I could, I skipped wiping the counters and sweeping the floor afterward. That done, I would run out to play.

One day I came up with a great invention. I carefully filled the frying pan and sauce pans with water and detergent, this time in smug anticipation that I was beating the system. Feeling as purposeful as the chemist Jack was, I put the pots in the oven and set it at 200 degrees. I figured the heat and soap would break up the grease and bits of food stuck to the pans and eliminate half the scrubbing for me.

While the pots simmered, I quickly washed the plates, silver and glasses, and placed each carefully in a rack on the drain board so that they would all fit in one load. Next, and here was what I thought was the genius of the scheme, I put the dish rack filled with clean, wet dishes outside the back door on a chair. The tiny landing went three steps down to our tiny, scraggly back yard. Realizing I had some time, I ran off to play and soon forgot about my task.

Hours later, my mother and Jack were sitting in the living room talking about the news and reading the paper. My mother lifted her head and sniffed. "There's a fishy smell, do you think?"

Jack harrumphed dismissively and continued reading. Finally my mother, huge in pregnancy, put her hands behind her on the arms of her chair, heaved herself up, belly forward, and went into the kitchen. The fumes were tangible as billowing clouds. Fearing a fire, she threw open the oven door and found the skillet and sauce pans bubbling away with bits of food and grease peeking through the suds.

She grabbed them with a potholder, placed them in the sink and opened the back door to let out the stench. There in front of her was one of the kitchen chairs and on it the dish rack filled with dishes. Except the dishes weren't clean. They had been washed all right, but they were now covered with cinders from the evening train that had roared by. Bits of leaves and gossamer threads from insects had caught onto the silverware and waved about willy-nilly.

"Sandy, whatever got into you? Did you think you could fool us by hiding the dishes?"

Neither of my parents believed I had invented a procedure that could spare American civilization unending work. I often ran into this problem where adults gave me more credit for being deliberately mischievous than for being a problem solver. There was no hope of convincing them that the great scientist was at work again.

"It would have worked." I protested tearfully. "The only problem was I forgot about them!" My mother made me wash the dishes all over again, dry them, and put them away. I learned my lesson, but to this day I hate household chores. They take away from time you can spend having fun.

THE PIGEON

My sister, Nancy, was born ten days before Christmas. Jack called her, *The Pigeon*, which was shortened to Pidge, because she looked like a fat capon. Jack was so excited about the birth of his first child he bought a big turkey on the day my mother came home from the hospital and invited friends over for dinner. My mother could hardly have been in great shape, but she baked the turkey and everyone celebrated.

Nancy was a great, big nine-pound baby and fit nicely into my arms. I was so happy to have a sister that I happily took care of her as much as possible. She slept in a crib in my parents' bedroom. It had bay windows with white lace curtains and looked out onto the street.

Often my mother let me sit there and rock Pidge in the wooden rocking chair until she fell asleep. She had colic and seemed to scream for hours. My mother was grateful that I took care of her, she had so many things to do, and I loved holding my sister and singing to her. As we swung back and forth in the rocking chair, I watched the shadows of the trees slide past the curtains when the buses went roaring by. Soon my sister would finally fall asleep. It was not long before Pidge preferred to come to my outstretched arms unless it was time for my mother to nurse her.

MERRY CHRISTMAS

After the move from New York, our family didn't have much money for Christmas. My mother took me aside for a conversation.

"We won't be able to give presents to each other this year, Sandy. Not even to you, even though you are a child, and you expect it."

Ten years old, I was crushed. For me, the whole point of Christmas was the presents. But there was nothing to do but accept it. I shut my mouth in a pout and let it go.

The day before Christmas, Jack called me to him.

"Sandy, I know we aren't giving presents, but don't you think we ought to surprise Mommy with a gift anyway? She is working so hard taking care of all of us and a new baby." *What? If anybody got a present, it should be me*, I thought. *Christmas is for kids.* I nodded my head sullenly.

Jack continued, "Let's go to Gray's Pharmacy and see what we can find." We put on our heavy winter coats and boots and walked to Dinky Town. Gray's was like today's CVS Drugstore, it stocked lots of attractive low-cost impulse items. Jack meandered up and down the aisles with me, and I followed behind, completely disinterested.

Jack stopped from time to time and held up various

items, a box of perfumed dusting powder, earrings, bath salts, a book, and asked, "Do you think Mommy would like this?"

Fighting feelings that I wasn't loved and that the whole thing was wrong-headed, I scowled, "I don't care."

Jack could not get me to cooperate with the project and finally bought a bottle of Evening in Paris, eau de toilette in its distinctive dark blue bottle. He had the store clerk wrap it up in store wrap, and we took it home and put it under the Christmas tree. It was the only present.

As had become a family tradition, we dressed up on Christmas Eve, and sat down in the dining room to a special dinner with our best tablecloth and dishes. Afterwards we had cake and ice cream, and my mother and Jack had coffee.

Then Jack said, "Let's go to the living room and open presents!"

I should have wondered why my mother agreed so readily. I sulkily got up and joined them. We all sat down around the tree, which was huge and decorated with colorful lights. Jack went over to it, squatted down and retrieved the solitary present wrapped up in drugstore paper without even a ribbon. Then he turned and walked over to me with a big smile on his face.

"Merry Christmas, Sandy. Mommy and I want you to have this."

I was overcome with shame and immediately realized that Jack and my mother had tried to get me to pick out a present for myself. Since there was only one, they wanted to make sure that it would be one I really wanted. I opened the gift slowly, knowing what was inside, and nearly choked on the words as I thanked them.

*　　*　　*

We didn't stay in Minneapolis long. Jack got a job as a lab tech at Bethesda Hospital in St. Paul, and we rented a second floor flat in the Capital Hill area. My mother and Jack joked that from our bathroom window we could see the four golden horses of the apocalypse that decorated the capitol dome. It was a small one-bedroom flat. I slept on the porch, which was painted white and had small framed panels of French windows on the three sides facing out. I loved the open window spaces and daydreamed as I looked up at the cloud formations and evening stars from my bed. The porch really wasn't considered a room and wasn't insulated like the rest of the house, so I slept in Jack's Army surplus, down sleeping bag.

I attended Sheffer School where I learned how to use a ruler and pencil to draw straight, parallel guide lines to help make an outline. We studied the three branches of government and the battles of the American Revolution.

Sandy with Pooch after fifth grade graduation, in back yard of house in SE, Minneapolis. My mother made the dress out of light blue organdy. I hadn't learned to act like a young lady in a dress yet.

ST PAUL, MINNESOTA

SUMMER THUNDERSHOWERS

WE LIVED IN several parts of the Twin Cities, when eventually my parents bought a large house in the black neighborhood of St. Paul. It was the only area where they could afford the mortgage. Coincidentally, it was the same neighborhood in which I had lived with Mrs. Williams and had gone to summer camp at Hallie Q. Brown, and the same neighborhood my mother and father had lived when they got married. The black community is small; it was also where my father had rented a room after they separated. There were commonalities over decades.

We moved into a double-porched duplex at 716 Carroll Avenue. Our house was huge, with high ceilings, five entrances, a full basement, and a full attic that could be converted into living space. In the summer the branches of the elm trees lining the street brushed up against the upstairs porch, lending the feeling we were in a treehouse. On hot, humid days in summer we sat up there and picnicked on potato salad. My parents drank beer and played cribbage while my sisters and I bounced up and down on the roll-away beds that doubled as couches.

When I lived with Mrs. Williams, my father's rooming house was just a few blocks away from our house on Carroll Avenue, down a few doors from the liquor store on the corner of Rondo and Dale Avenue. This was a heralded corner over many years and is part of the local history of the neighborhood. Men loitered there, casually holding their small pint bottles of liquor by the neck, not very well disguised in a brown paper bag, and taking a sip from time to time. Unemployed, they passed the time talking and smoking and idly watching the people as they passed by. By the time we moved to Carroll Avenue, however, my father was living in Chicago.

In high school I walked up Rondo past the house where my father had roomed, to Dale, just a block over from our house on Carroll, and then down Dale Avenue a mile to University Avenue where I caught a crosstown bus to the University in Minneapolis, where I took ballet lessons at the Andahazy Ballet School, located not far from the entrance to the campus.

At the same time, I settled in with a circle of black friends during junior high and high school. In 1955, my sister, Ann, was born. She was tiny, and the cuddliest baby I've ever held. She was so easy to take care of, I thought of her as an angel. At last, I had a family with two baby sisters, Pooch, of course, and a piano. It wasn't until this time, when my mother remarried, bought a home and creat-ed a real family that my life finally settled down. I stopped fighting, followed the college track in high school, and brought home good grades.

Around March, as soon as the temperature rose

above freezing, I took Jack's army-surplus down sleeping bag and slept outside on the upstairs porch as witness to the coming of spring. At first the tree branches were stark and spare. Then small, pale, green buds appeared, so subtle I thought they could only be seen from my bird's eye view up in my eyrie. Because the season is short, spring pushes in powerfully in Minnesota. Tight little buds leafed out within weeks to the full, green bower that surrounded our upstairs porch.

Thunderstorms accompany the swift onset of a Minnesota summer, filling the intersection at the end of our block waist-high with water. The storm drains were rarely cleared during the year and were clogged with last fall's leaves and assorted refuse.

I loved the rain. First of all, it was a relief from the muggy heat. But there was also something magical about immersing myself in the showers of a summer storm. All of us kids on the block played in the rain, jumping into puddles and running around until our shorts and t-shirts were soaked. Gradually we would discover the little lake at the end of the street at the intersection of Carroll Avenue and St. Albans Street and run down and dive around in the murky water.

The adults told us never to play in the rain, particularly when there was lightning because we could get electrocuted, but I wasn't sure I believed them. Their warnings sounded more like they were trying to scare us into not swimming and having fun in the (filthy) pool of water. We kids were not aware of the refuse, the occasional dead rat, or the cigarette butts that floated in our idyllic pond. What we saw was a pristine lake surrounded by trees and houses right in the middle of our little city. Its occurrence was as magical as a rainbow suddenly appearing from nowhere. We splashed each other and tried to run in the water, occasionally ducking under and pulling each other down while the rain streamed down our faces, blurring our vision and my glasses.

I am aware now that the world I lived in as a kid must have been very different from the one defined by the concerns of my parents. We each lived in our little sphere of place, coexisting with each other but actually participating in quite different lives.

12

ST PAUL, MINNESOTA

Sandy, Nancy and Ann in polka dot dresses our mother sewed for us for Easter. 1956

LOCKED OUT

WE HAD A NUMBER of adventures when my mother and stepfather went to visit friends in New York one summer and entrusted me with the responsibility of taking care of my two sisters. I had just turned 14, and my sisters were two and four years old, respectively. We still lived in the great, big two-story, five bedroom house on Carroll Avenue in St. Paul, right in the middle of the black community. We had moved in when I was eleven. It was the first real home we had ever owned, and it remains an idyllic memory for me and my sisters.

That summer, my parents decided to drive our little blue VW Beetle to New York City to see friends and family. We had moved out of our apartment in the Bronx six years earlier when I was nine years old. At fourteen, I was immature, certainly not ready to take care of a house and family, but that summer I had already taken on responsibilities involved in taking care of my sisters while my parents worked and attended classes. Eventually, my mother would earn a Masters in library science and my stepfather a masters degree in chemistry.

They discussed the trip to New York longingly. It would be kind of a vacation from hard work, graduate school, and family. My parents' eagerness to see their old friends clouded their good judgment.

They decided that I could take care of my two sisters and reassured themselves that I was up to it. After all, I was already the designated babysitter and was doing the many chores that go along with being at home—laundry, vacuuming, cooking. What could go wrong? The neighbors would keep an ear out, they rationalized, if anything serious should happen. A callow youth, I had no qualms and agreed to babysit for the ten days because my parents promised to bring back a stupendous present for me. I imagined trendy clothes like a full skirt, a tight sweater or Capezio flats from New York's famous garment district.

With school out, I was certainly available to take care of my sisters. Babysitting, my parents reasoned, was not much less responsibility than taking care of the family full-time. With a promise to buy me a special present, my parents packed up the Volskwagen and drove off.

In my mind the only hard part would be being alone in the house at night. Right off the bat I locked all the doors. When my parents were in town we had never locked them, but I was a little spooked that a robber would come in while we were out, and we would return not knowing he was there.

One day I planned to take my sisters and walk the five or six blocks to my friend's house for a visit. Everyone walked in those days, and it was easy to carry Ann when she got tired. I loved my little sisters and was happy to take them everywhere. My friends liked them, too. They were shy and quiet and no trouble at all. That afternoon I dutifully locked the front and back doors as we left the house. But I forgot to take the key with me. It was lying on the dining room table. We had left in such a flurry of activity that I had forgotten to pick up the key and put it in my pocket.

When we returned home at the end of a long day, having walked to my friend's house, gone to a local school playground, hanging around, and walking home again, we were tired and eager to get inside and rest. It was then that I realized we were locked out. There was no way to climb in the windows because they were high off the ground and had screens on them. I went around to each of the entrances and sure enough, the house was more secure than Fort Knox.

Standing in front with my two sisters I gazed up at the huge house and started thinking. My eyes went to the treetops brushing up against the top porch shrouding it in leafy boughs, and I looked further up to the windows in the attic. A sliver of space revealed that one of the attic windows was open, and I hit on a practical solution. "What I need is a ladder," I mused. "I could get in through the attic and come downstairs and open the door."

Quick as a bunny I went next door and asked if I could use their phone.

"Sandy Rogers," I identified myself. It was clear from my voice that I was a kid. "I need a fire truck with a big ladder."

The dispatcher was trained to waste no words and asked for no explanation. She naturally assumed there was a fire.

"What is your address?"

I told her we lived at 716 Carroll Avenue and the only way in was through the attic.

Within minutes a huge hook and ladder truck came roaring up the street accompanied by a smaller fire engine and a police car. The vehicles came to a stop in front of our house. My sisters and I were standing in front under the elm tree. I greeted them, "Oh, thank you for coming!"

Six or seven firemen all decked out in fire gear jumped off the truck as it drew to a stop. Turning to me, the leader asked, "You made the call?"

"Yes!" I pointed, "Up there, put the ladder up there."

The fireman nodded and proceeded to unfold the ladder from the truck, pivot it around, and leaned it against the porch, positioned to get in the upstairs attic window.

"Thanks," I said, and started to climb the ladder. But one of the firemen grabbed me by the upper arm and pulled me away.

"It's not safe," he said. "We'll handle it," and a couple of firemen immediately scurried up the ladder.

The firemen were all business and did not talk to me. I noticed the whole crew was bristling with efficiency as they set about their jobs like busy ants in their highly organized community. In the short time that I was admiring their team work, two firemen went through the house and came crashing out the through front door.

"Where is the fire!" they yelled at me. "We can't find the fire!"

For the first time I had the full attention of the firemen. Peering through my thick coke-bottle glasses and holding my sisters' hands, I patiently explained that we were locked out, and I knew they had long ladders which could reach high enough for me to get in the house to open the door. Exasperated, the firemen looked at each other and then at me.

"Do you realize how much money it costs to go out on a fire call?" They chastised me in terse words, packed up their hoses, folded up the ladder and drove away. The neighbors who had by this time gathered to watch the commotion, also turned and went back in their homes.

When my parents came home from New York, I told them about this adventure, thinking they would be proud of me for my resourcefulness. They listened with a combination of chagrin and mild amusement. A few weeks later they received a bill from the city for $150, quite a lot of money in those days.

APPLE PIES

While my parents were in New York, a kindly neighbor gave us a bushel of apples and, realizing that they might go rotten before we ate them all, I decided to make a bunch of apple pies. I prepared the crusts, sliced the apples, added brown sugar, cinnamon, a bit of lemon and every Minnesotan's secret ingredient, butter, and put the pies in the oven. The phone rang in the dining room next to the kitchen just as I turned on the gas from the pilot light underneath the oven. The call was from one of my girlfriends. Those were the days when teenagers talked for hours on the phone. While we talked, I completely forgot that the gas was running. We talked and laughed and gossiped for a long time.

"Girl!"

And I said, "Really?!"

"You know it. That's how it happened. . ."

We must have talked for over an hour.

When I got off the phone I caught a whiff of gas that by that time had filled the kitchen. Mindful that the pilot light from the refrigerator could ignite a conflagration, I was frightened that the house would blow up. I told my two sisters to stay well back in the living room while I fixed the problem. Something in my tone must have made them sense my fear. I looked over my shoulder from the kitchen through the dining room into the living room where they were huddled and made sure they were obeying me. Pidge and Ann were crouched behind a couch with their little blond heads stuck out, straining to see what I was doing. Our dog, Pooch, sat panting on the floor next to them, his tongue lolling in a wide grin.

Confident that I was doing what any mature adult would do, I squatted down in front of the oven thinking furiously, *I have to get rid of this gas, and now.* I swiftly decided to just burn it off. I reached up and grabbed the box of stick matches from the top of the stove, intent on taking care of the problem.

Scratch! Went the match against the side of the box, followed immediately by a gigantic, Boom! There was a huge explosion, and I was immediately enveloped in a plume of flame that filled the kitchen. Then, just as suddenly, it stopped. Everyone in the house, including Pooch, was still. *Well,* I thought, as I made sure the gas was off, that's done. *We saved the house.*

It was then that I looked down and saw the skin hanging off my right forearm that I had used to strike the match. I realized that my arm was stinging with a burning pain. I thought about it and called 911 (emergency).

"We just had a fire. Will you give me the phone number of a hospital?"

The operator quickly connected me to an emergency room, and I asked the nurse what I should do for a very bad burn. Being a kid, I did not say that I was in the middle of a huge explosion or that the skin was hanging off my arm. Actually, I found out later that my face was also burned and my eyebrows and eyelashes had been singed. The nurse, to whom I had not really given enough information, said there really wasn't anything to do, just keep the wound clean and put ice on it. The burn was so bad that I rested my entire arm in a roaster pan filled with ice water and carried it around with me for several days.

When my parents came home from New York, they brought me a present, just as they promised. It was a Bulova watch. I was disappointed that it wasn't clothes, but they assured me that a Bulova was the best and it was worth fifty dollars. I didn't catch on that they must have gotten it at a discounted price and accepted the caché of my expensive new present. The only feedback my sisters gave my parents was that all they had to eat while Mama and Jack were gone was apple pie.

ST PAUL, MINNESOTA

PIECES OF A MAP

BY THE TIME I WAS FIFTEEN I had never lived in any one place as long as I had in our house on Carroll Avenue, and although my life had stabilized, it was still a complex weave of disparate cultures. First, there was my nuclear family— my white mother, Jewish stepfather, white sisters, and our dog. Then, there was the black community in which we lived, and my African American girlfriends with whom I identified. With the exception of Jack, who declared himself an atheist, we all went to church, which contributed to our value systems.

Just as it had from the times of slavery the black church preached civil rights and negotiating the evils of racial discrimination as part of a paradigm for right living. The church was a relevant institution in those days. My set of girlfriends went to Central High, which was college oriented and socially stratified: The jocks ate in one part of the cafeteria, the popular girls in another, and we black girls kept together as well. Very few black kids attended Central High. Most of the kids in our neighborhood went to its rival, Mechanic Arts.

Jack bought me a Raleigh bicycle, and I joined the American Youth Hostels and pedaled around Minnesota with the University folk dancers. Every week I took a city bus on University Avenue from St. Paul to Minneapolis and folk-danced at the U of M student union. Afterwards the dancers took me with them to a local bar where they had beers even though I was under age. I didn't drink. I never got into drinking. Alcohol tasted like medicine to me, and I was able to get crazy happy on my own, without alcohol. Sometimes after folk dancing on a hot summer night, we drove to one of the local lakes and went skinny-dipping.

The folk dancers also took me camping and on canoe trips in Minnesota's North Woods, where we danced until the wee hours of the morning. On one winter trip, we took a sauna and then, our bare feet skidding on the snowy path, ran to a frozen river and jumped in through a hole we cut in the ice. It was exhilarating for exactly three seconds, and then we scrambled out of the river and back to the sauna, only to repeat the process again

One time we went to a Serbo-Croatian folk dance festival in Northern Minnesota, and a person asked if I were a Croatian Negro. I danced with gusto and loved the strong line dances and powerful music of Serbia, Russia, and Yugoslavia. Its proud, defiant spirit expressed my need for respect. We were all Negroes. When I grew up, my goal was to join a Russian folk dance troupe..

I was also involved in social activities associated with my mother's political work. These included civil rights and peace marches, Socialist Workers meetings, potluck dinners at White Bear Lake, and League of Women Voters discussions. The people in our neighborhood considered our family interesting, a bit unusual. Mixed-race families were an anomaly in those days.

The social groups I was a part of did not overlap. Each was populated by a different set of people of varying ages and orientations. I was used to being thrust into a variety of cultures and situations and having to adapt to each. It was a matter of survival. My mother must have been sensitive to the juggling I had to do to fit in and once told me that to be a truly integrated individual you must be the same person in every situation you find yourself. I tried to follow her advice but compensated by acting wild and trying to make people laugh.

There was another family that was as much of an oddity in the community as ours. The Schultzes. They lived about six blocks from our house, and shared a special bond with us. I think it was because both our families were driven by politically idealistic thinking. When Leon Trotsky visited the United States from the Soviet Union, he declared Henry Schultz the best union organizer in the country. Henry and Dorothy had four children. Henry was a brilliant man, but he drank heavily, and his thoughts had taken a dark, angry turn by the time he entered my life. Dorothy Schultz and my mother were similar in several ways. Both were generous, quiet, and soft-spoken. They were both librarians and intellectuals, and the central force in each family. Our families were similarly configured around our mothers.

The Schultzes had four children. Ann was five years older than I— I saw little of her. Jim, the next oldest, was my age. He and I walked the same route to John Marshall Jr. High, his jeans belted low on his hips at the precise point where they could slip off, much like kids who "sag" their pants today. Jim and I had nothing to do with each other. He ran around with a bunch of white boys, swearing, smoking cigarettes and causing trouble, and I walked with my coterie of black girl friends. No one would have guessed we knew each other. Jim was always getting suspended from school for fighting. Later, he went on to Mechanic Arts, while I went to Central High. Jim was brilliant like his father. His younger brothers, twins, Vince and Ray, were named after Vincent Raymond Dunne, one of the founders of the American Communist Party.

The very first time our family went to their house, Vince and Ray came tumbling out of the front door, down the steps and rolled around on the grass fighting. I liked them immediately.

St. Paul Youth Couuncil Still Picket Woolworth's

Picketing Woolworths, 1960.   Vincent Schultz is holding the sign at the far right in front. Raymond Schultz is standing behind me on the left.

Socialist Workers' Party campaign headquarters, 540 Cedar
Street, St. Paul, 1946. Picture from front page of Minneapolis Tribune.

Grace Carlson (right) and an unidentified woman leaving SWP headquarters during the raid. Picture from Minneapolis Tribune, June 28, 1941.

Socialist Workers Party picnic, 1950.
L to R: Vincent Ray Dunne, Dorothy Schultz, Henry Schultz, and
Carl Skogland, one of the leaders of the 1934 Minneapolis Teamsters
strikes.

The Schultzes were union organizers and Socialists deeply committed to improving economic conditions for the poor. In 1946 Dorothy Schultz ran for Congress for the Socialist Party. They may have crossed paths with my mother and father at the time because the Hallie Q. Brown settlement house was the focus of the civil rights work in the black community. Dorothy's sister, Grace Carlson, ran for Senate on the same ticket. In a raid on the Socialist Workers Party headquarters in St. Paul, Dorothy and Grace were arrested and indicted for, "advocating the overthrow of the government through force and violence." Portraits of Lenin and Trotsky, pamphlets, and books for sale were seized as evidence in the raid.

Grace Carlson, Vincent Ray Dunne, Carl Skogland and fifteen other Socialist Workers Party Trotskyites were the first to be sentenced under the Alien Registration Act— the Smith Act of 1940. Grace and her husband were sent to prison as part of the first efforts to discourage political dissent leading to the McCarthy era. When I heard the adults regaling each other with stories about their organizing days, I remembered Julius and Ethel Rosenberg, whose kids I was worried about when I was a little girl in New York. The Rosenbergs were executed as Soviet spies during the height of the McCarthy era. Grace was a folk hero in our family because she had gone to jail for her beliefs, still a badge of honor for politicos today.

Our families often got together for dinner, taking turns gathering at each other's home. On these occasions we kids would run all over the house, chasing and having fun while the adults discussed politics. Often Phil and Joan Brum, also socialist politicos, came with their children.

There was always an argument between the Schultzes and the Brums: Should we change the country through violent revolution or should we work from within, politically? It was the Leninists against the Trotskyites. My mother didn't enter the fray. While supportive of socialist principles, she was an ardent pacifist; her position on the matter was clear.

The political arguments were vitriolic, and we kids skirted the living room where the adults were drinking beer and whiskey and connecting their case to the political events of the day. By this time, in the late 1950s, the Socialist Workers Party was moving to the right toward middle class protest politics. Henry and Dorothy remained Trotskyites, however, and the SWP party eventually stripped them of their responsibilities, rendering them politically inactive. This may have been part of the reason Henry Schultz was such a bitter man.

Towards the end of the evening when the adults were mellow with good food and alcohol, we sang political songs that reflected nostalgia for the good fight and bygone times. One satirical camp song was catchy:

Hey Lenin, hey Trotsky, we're the Russian diplomotski,
You have a meeting with the czar-ar-ar!
We have traveled near and far-ar-ar!

Hen Len, hey Trot, we're the Russian diplomots
Hey peesha, pasha, pusha, prussia,
Hell's bells, hey!

We sang union songs like *There Will Be Pie in the Sky When You Die, Solidarity Forever* and *Put it On the Ground:*

Chorus:
    Oh, Mr. Hackenpacker, what should we do?
    We don't earn enough money to take care of our families!
Mr. Hackenpacker:
    Oh! If you want a raise in pay, all you have to do,
    Go and ask the boss for it and he will give it to you
    Yes, he will give it to you, my boys,
    He will give it to you
    A raise in pay, without delay, oh, he will give it to you.
Chorus:
    Ohhh, put it on the ground, spread it all around
    Dig it with a hoe: it will make your flowers grow!

My life was a mélange of cultures, political ideas, and religious orientations. Adapting to each was like learning to be conversant in a different language, like placing the pieces of a puzzle into a large map. I enjoyed exploring and integrating these pieces of my life. It broadened my perspective and, eventually, I was able to make one coherent world of it.

ST PAUL, MINNESOTA

Sandy, sophomore in high school, 1958.

DOING WELL IN HIGH SCHOOL

MY TEENAGE YEARS WERE SPENT doing the kinds of things adolescents do. It's a queer breed, teenagers. I was intensely vulnerable, moody and felt passionately misunderstood. This was not a time to distinguish myself from the herd. I fiercely wanted to belong to a group and happily tried to be just like my best friends. We packed a little overnight bag with a housecoat and pajamas when we spent the night at each other's house, we dressed alike, and we practiced witty comebacks, called, "capping."

My friends were raised in the heart of black tradition, learned about their culture and took pride in it. My situation was different. As the only black kid in an all-white family I had to play catch-up, learning what it meant to be black by being respectful of elders, appreciating green beans and pork chop sandwiches, and fast-dancing with the boys. We were also expected to do well in school.

In high school I took the classes that were expected of me. My mother sniffed with contempt when I wanted to take Home Economics, saying it wasn't real education. Instead, each year I followed the sequence of courses in English, history, math, French, and science. I continued this pattern in college, ending up with a double major in math and philosophy and double minors in French and political science.

I wasn't any good at science, I just didn't catch on. In 11th grade I took chemistry. I caught onto the symbols and nomenclature, but I hadn't a clue what the fundamentals of chemistry were. Since Jack was a chemist, I asked him for help. He wasn't a good fit as a tutor. He had no patience with me and just repeated the definition of a term in the same dense vocabulary that it was presented.

"I don't get it. What is an enzyme?"

"An enzyme is a substance produced by a living organism which acts as a catalyst to bring about a biochemical reaction." He spoke from real familiarity with the subject and sounded bored that he had to repeat it to me.

It was circular, you needed to know the meaning of a word to understand its meaning, and none of the words meant anything to me. I had no operational understanding of what he was saying. Nowadays, teachers provide physical experiences to engage students and help them create content for new concepts. I suspected Jack thought I was dumb, and I that I somehow couldn't learn chemistry. We mutually agreed to quit working together.

In chemistry lab one time, I accidentally dissolved my synthetic Orlon acrylic sweater. While I didn't understand chemistry, I did enjoy the lab, handling the equipment, pouring, stirring, and using Bunson burners. I talked eagerly with my friends and sailed through my experiments without a care for safety. Hydrochloric acid looks like water, but is lighter, less viscous. Standing at my station, I snatched a beaker of twelve normal HCl, hyrodrochloric acid, from the shelf in front of me. The acid splashed up and out, all over my sweater. To my horror, my sweater dissolved in front of my eyes, revealing my white slip trimmed with lace and my utilitarian white cotton 32AA bra. I was mortified and didn't even notice the stinging on my face.

My teacher, Mr. Ring told me to go to the bathroom to rinse it off and added that it was lucky I was wearing glasses.

The next year, in 12th grade, I took physics. This was even less fathomable to me than chemistry. There were about twelve boys in the class. I was the only girl, and the only black kid. The group was small, and the teacher, Mr. Brett, really loved science. The boys enjoyed a great rapport with him. I couldn't follow any of it. I had never worked on cars, built bicycles, or looked at electrical circuits, as many boys had been exposed to at home.

Mr. Brett saw I was floundering, and realized I was headed toward failing the class. He invited me to stay after school as a lab assistant. My job was to put away equipment and organize materials. While doing so, I could ask him questions and get some tutoring. Some of the boys also stayed after school, working on their science projects. The mood in the lab was festive and industrious. One group of boys trained a rocket they were building out an open window of the lab which was on the third floor and accidentally launched it. It made a huge boom, and startled me, but they all laughed with pleasure.

My physics project was to build a cloud chamber. It was suggested to me by Larry Petersen, who was a physicist. He and his wife were friends of the family and came to dinner from time to time. I was intrigued by the concept of a "cloud chamber," and listened carefully as Larry explained it to me. Basically, I put a lot of frozen carbon dioxide, CO_2 in a glass terrarium and somehow, when you shined a flashlight in, you could see evidence of some ions, which proved the existence of radiation.

I built the cloud chamber at home and went through the procedure a number of times. I thought about the leftover frozen carbon dioxide and remembered that plants get CO_2 from the air and release oxygen into the atmosphere. My mother had plants and ferns all over the house, and I reasoned that they provided fresh air in a house that was well insulated against the cold during Minnesota's long winters. I was happy thinking about this. Everything fit together, and I got a brainstorm. I would help Mama's plants by sticking little bits of leftover CO_2 the size of small hail stones, beneath the soil around the roots of her plants. I did this and then put away the equipment until my next practice when I would write up my results.

About a week later my mother said to Jack, "I don't understand it. All my plants have died."

Sitting at the table in the dining room, I looked up at the enormous bush of a fern plant in front of the bay window. It was indeed dead. It had turned a decisive brown. I had never really paid attention to Mama's plants before, but as I looked around, the African violets, philodendrons, spider plants and ferns that my mother had placed all over the house had withered away and died. I told her about my attempt to provide them with a boost and she sighed and shook her head at me in disappointment.

TELEVISION

During the time I was a teenager television was finding its way into the living rooms of American homes as a cultural institution. We had two television sets in the living room of our house on Carroll Avenue. One was a handsome console, which had sound, but no picture, and on top of it, we placed a smaller television whose picture projected from a ten-inch screen My parents watched the evening news with Walter Cronkite, and Jack looked forward to the Friday night fights. Jack loved all sports and was pretty good at stick ball and soft ball. He might have done more with sports, but a heart condition prevented him. It also kept him out of the army. Jack loved football, the

Chicago Bears were his favorite team. He would sit on the edge of the couch, yelling and cheering, fairly leaping off the couch while still in a sitting position. As he punched the air alternately cheering and castigating his team, my mother would pass by, on her way to the kitchen, and quietly demur, "Football is a barbaric sport."

They also watched, "Gunsmoke," the "Ed Sullivan Show," and "Dragnet." But, I didn't watch television. We couldn't afford one when I was young, and by the time I became a teenager, I was more interested in being with my friends.

DRIVING

When I was fifteen I got my driver's license. This turned out to be a good thing for my mother. She let me drive to my friends' houses if I would take my sister with me. I felt responsible driving our light blue VW bug around the neighborhood, and it gave her a little time to do things she needed to take care of. My sisters were shy and did not demand attention. I was proud to have my little sisters with me, and they idolized my teenage friends as we talked and laughed, practiced fast dancing to rhythm and blues records, and made bacon and toast sandwiches.

Our VW was built economically and had no gas gauge. When you ran out of gas you were supposed to release a lever, which would give you another gallon of gas from an auxiliary tank, enough to get to a filling station. One day I was driving around, running errands for my mother and visiting friends, and I ran out of gas. I pulled the auxiliary lever and thought no more about it.

The next day, when Jack drove to work in Stillwater, about 30 miles from our house, he ran out of gas. It was awful because it was winter and the temperature was below zero. Jack had to hike through the snow on the side of the road until someone picked him up and took him to a gas station. It was one of the few times that Jack was really angry with me.

FIRST JOB

Also, when I was fifteen, I got my first job working Saturdays as a cashier at a barber school in downtown St. Paul. I took a city bus to the storefront at the ragged edge of the business and shopping district. My cashier's station was positioned in the middle of a long room and faced windows looking out on Roberts Street. From my stool I could see customers and denizens of the depressed area passing by on the sidewalk.

The barber school was brown and dank, smelling of stale hair tonic and the cheap fragrance of foaming shaving cream. Shorn hair covered the floor in clumps, and tiny bits of hair flew all around. Imagining they were sticking to my face, I fanned the air in front of me with my hand. Along the two facing walls were a succession of barber chairs in which the customers sat. Our clients were ordinary working men, students, and an occasional bum who wanted a cleanup.

A haircut cost 85 cents, and a shave 40 cents. I quickly learned to do the mental math to make change, scooping nickels and quarters expertly from the cashier's drawer. The most common transaction was subtracting 85 cents from a dollar or $1.25 from two dollars. I enjoyed handling the coins and quickly learned the possible combinations of nickels, dimes, quarters and half-dollars. At lunch I crossed Roberts Street and went to a greasy spoon where I sat on a stool at the counter and ordered a grilled cheese sandwich and a glass of milk. I felt very grown up.

A friend of the family did this abstract painting of me. My mother felt it captured my teenage anger and defiance.

ST PAUL, MINNESOTA

ICE CUBES

MY MOTHER NEVER spanked me. She was a pacifist. When I was a little girl and got in trouble, stole, or fought, she sat me in her lap and talked to me about it. She patiently explained why what I had done was wrong. My misbehavior made her sorrowful, and her tone was soft and compassionate. At these times I couldn't understand what made her so sad. From my point of view wrongdoing was ubiquitous.

This is why I was caught completely by surprise one morning when my mother whirled around from the kitchen sink, her eyes blazing behind her glasses, and she threw a tray of ice cubes in my face.

The incident happened when I was in high school. Actually, it had all started a few years before. My stepfather, Jack, and I were best buddies when I was a little girl. He married my mother when I was nine, and he and I cavorted around pretending we were gangsters, shooting water pistols at each other, and acting like kids. We had watermelon-seed and cherry-pit spitting fights, and yelled and chased each other around our apartment in the Bronx, and even our house on Carroll Avenue. Jack was seven years younger than my mother, marrying her when he was 28. He was a natural prankster and closer to me in some ways than he was to the responsible world my mother had lived in since she was very young. If a kid hit me or insulted me, Jack insisted I fight back and defend myself. He helped turn me into an all-around hellion.

Jack praised me for my antics in school and encouraged me to challenge my teachers verbally and to speak up for my ideas. Once he and my mother attended a lecture by the award winning physicist, George Gamov, who had worked on the Big Bang theory. During the lecture, Jack stood up and pointed out a mistake Gamov had made on the chalkboard. Amazingly, Gamov graciously accepted the correction and continued on with his lecture while my mother shrank down in her chair and tried to become invisible.

Our relationship worked fine until I became a teenager. By this time we were living in the black neighborhood of St. Paul. I didn't realize it, but something had changed in me. I was turning into a girly-girl. I changed my clothes a couple of times a day, each time throwing my entire outfit into the laundry. I needed privacy, and I became touchy emotionally. If only I had known that all this was part of adolescence.

But Jack continued his fun-loving antics. His pranks tortured me. When my friends came over, he greeted them with, "Have you been running? You smell tired!" A few years earlier this query would have triggered a peal of laughter, but in front of my girlfriends, with whom it was very important that I not only be accepted, but that I be identical in every way, I was mortified. He was a wise cracker, but having heard all his jokes over and over again, I no longer thought them funny.

Jack made fun of me, too, and called me Shmegegge, which means, an idiot. I had entered a stage when I doubted myself, and I felt that he, who had received straight A's through high school and college, had lost faith in me, too. Shmegegge hurt.

* * *

My girlfriends and I were considered good girls in the black community. We went to church, earned good grades in school, and called each other's mothers, "Untee Ruby," and "Untee Bea." We did household chores and were paragons of virtue. So, it was natural, when professional and college football or basketball players came to town, they wanted to date my set of friends because we were nice.

One year Carl Eller, a football player at the University of Minnesota who went on to become a member of the NFL Vikings, invited me to his homecoming dance. I was excited at the prospect. Sandy Stephens and Alan Page, also football players, invited my girlfriends.

My mother sewed a beautiful teal blue dress for me. It had a princess waistline and a pleated boat-wing collar, and I wore four-inch black patent leather high heels and suntan-shaded nylon stockings. This was enormous. The evening of our date arrived, and I was all ready, probably very pretty, even with my glasses with thick, coke-bottle lenses. Carl came to the house and rang the bell. I greeted him at the door and let him in.

There was a certain etiquette expected in the community. The boy comes over and meets the parents of the girl, and they all sit down in the living room and engage in polite conversation. Carl was six-foot six inches tall and weighed 247 pounds, a giant, as he stood in the doorway. He towered over me, who, at five-foot seven, was the tallest person in my family. Jack took a step back, tipped his round, red-cheeked face up, and said in admiration, "Wow! You are a monster! What size shoe do you wear?" Jack was a sports enthusiast and followed football, baseball and boxing religiously. I didn't realize it at the time, but he was probably looking forward as much to seeing Carl as I was.

Carl was taken aback. Did, "monster," coming from this short, round white man reference his race? White people were always disrespecting black folk. Carl was expecting to meet a black family. "How are you?" and, "So nice to see you— how do you like Minnesota?" was the conversation he was prepared to engage in. He mumbled that his shoes were a size 13. Carl had not been asked to sit down yet, so we all continued to stand awkwardly in the living room. Then Jack started dancing around like a boxer, hunching his shoulders up and down and feinting punches. He challenged Carl, "Hit me! Hit me! Bet you can't land one."

Now Carl was really in a pickle. If he even tapped my stepfather, he might have knocked him down. He stood there, frozen. Jack, thumbing his nose, sniffing, continued dancing lightly on the balls of his feet. Because of his height, his punches jabbed at Carl's midsection, which would have been comical if it weren't humiliating. My mother resolved the situation by inviting Carl to sit and offering him a beverage. That's what we used to say in the neighborhood, "Would you like a beverage?"

So, that was the beginning. Jack endlessly embarrassed me in front of my friends.

Our big eleven-room, two-story house had old plumbing. If the toilet was flushed on the first floor, anyone taking a shower upstairs would be spiked with scalding hot water from the change in water pressure. Once, when I had my well-raised girlfriends over, Jack came downstairs outraged, stark naked, and dripping wet. He stood in a puddle of water and roared, "Who flushed the goddamn toilet?"

One of my friends who had just used the bathroom

off the kitchen was terribly embarrassed. Seeing that I had company, Jack turned on his heel and stalked back upstairs. He wasn't embarrassed to be seen naked, but he knew it wasn't proper.

My family was talked about from one end of the neighborhood to the other. Finally, when I was fifteen, I had had enough. I decided that Jack was an animal. His earthy jokes were shocking to my teenage sensibilities.

One time he said to a pair of nuns who were visiting, "May I ask you a question?"

"Certainly," the nuns replied. "Anything."

"Is it true you don't have sex?"

They assented that the Church was their only husband. Then Jack asked, "How do you do it?"

In the strained silence that followed, my mother, sitting next to him on the couch with her back straight, wrung her hands and said temperately, "Now, Jack . . ."

Not everything that Jack did bothered me. He really enjoyed his family, and I took this for granted.

Sometimes he would say, "Come on, Mommy, let's go upstairs and play a game of chest!" They did often play chess together, but this wasn't what he meant. Jack would then throw her over his shoulder and carry my mother upstairs. I didn't pay much attention to this, but my sisters would follow them and come back smiling a little while later to giggle as they reported.

"Daddy's tickling Mommy again."

By the time I was fifteen, Jack's jokes were tiresome. When I asked him for money to go to the movies with my friends, he would roll over on one hip in his chair, reach into his pocket and say, "Sure!" Then he made a great show of digging around and pulling out some change, which he would slowly sort out in the palm of his hand. With a wicked grin he would offer a nickel to me saying, "Is this enough?" I had to plead with him to give me the fifty-cent price of admission. If I asked for another quarter to buy popcorn and a drink, he would protest loudly, "What?!" and start up again. Sometimes I got so mad I just wrangled with him for the price of admission and skipped any hope of getting enough money for refreshments.

*   *   *

I lectured my mother about how to handle the situation, a practice of mine since childhood. When I was five, I nagged at her that she should find a good father for me and make us a whole family. To help her out, I asked handsome young men on the subway or on busses if they would like to be my daddy. They loved it. I had provided the pickup line they needed to meet a beautiful blond, blue-eyed Minnesotan. Sometimes they gave me a quarter and a smile, which made me even more vigilant about not missing an opportunity to introduce my mother to a handsome man, despite her chiding me that it was not a good idea. I patiently explained to my mother that Jack was too gross and vulgar to be in our family and that he embarrassed me to tears.

I had explained this on multiple occasions until that fateful Saturday morning when my mother was defrosting the refrigerator. She walked back and forth from the refrigerator to the sink with me trailing after her, yammering away about why she should divorce Jack. She may have been irritated that I wasn't helping, but I was oblivious, pressing my case about why Jack was intolerable.

I had no idea of the pressures my mother was under, getting up at 4:00 in the morning to study for a masters in library science, working full-time as a librarian in South St. Paul, managing the house, and taking care of three children, a husband and a dog. I didn't realize that parents never have time off from their responsibilities or that they aren't completely able to dedicate all their attention to the needs and wants of their children. There was a queer connection here. My life oddly paralleled my mother's in some ways. When I was in my forties, I also got up at 4:00 in the morning, ahead of my kids and husband, to study and run with the dogs before going to work.

That Saturday morning in the kitchen my mother

reached a breaking point. She whirled around from the kitchen sink, her eyes blazing behind her glasses and turned with such force that the ice cubes in the tray she was defrosting flew in my face.

"Will you shut up?" she shouted.

That was the only act of physical violence I ever witnessed from my mother. It was so out of character, that I was taken aback, but my feelings weren't hurt.

"Gee, I don't see why you have to get so mad," I muttered as I left the kitchen. There was a lot I would have to learn before I grew up.

Jack wasn't all bad. He actually gave me much more than I gave him credit for at the time, and nowadays I refer to him as my father because he filled that role for me.

ST PAUL, MINNESOTA

RACISM

MY SISTERS' SKIN IS WHITE as snow. Nancy, has that clear, china-white skin whose fine blue veins only enhance its beauty. When I was young I thought she could be a model in a Breck shampoo ad. My other sister, Ann's, complexion was like peaches and cream. Both my sisters are beautiful, and I adored them. Even at a young age I knew I was black and they were white, but it didn't matter.

I had experienced racism at school and on the streets. I was a black child raised by a white mother in white neighborhoods until she and my stepfather bought our house in the black community of St. Paul. But there were no incidents of racism in our family. My sisters never called me nigger. Of course, they were ten years younger than I, and spent most of their childhood idealizing me as a teenager. I took care of them after school and summers because my parents worked and could not afford a babysitter. I loved taking care of them. They were my real family. I had waited ten years to get a father and mother, two sisters and a dog. I doted on them, taught them to play bridge and took them everywhere with me.

When I grew up, I and taught in an innovative 24-hour school that was part of the Synanon Foundation in Marin County. One night I was putting Bonnie, a beautiful five-year old with blue eyes and yellow-gold ringlets to bed.

We teachers were close to our students and close friends with their parents. We all lived together in an intentional community. We woke the kids in the morning, got them dressed and breakfasted, and then taught a stringent academic curriculum. At the end of the day we bathed the children, read stories, and put them to bed. We modeled their upbringing on the kibbutz.

It was at this time one warm, fall evening when I was tucking Bonnie into bed, that she snuggled into her covers, looked up at me and asked, "Sandy, do you hate being brown?"

"No, of course, not," I answered. I paused a moment and continued, "I like it. We are all different colors."

We were sharing a moment of closeness before falling asleep. Bonnie had asked out of love, but there was concern in her face as well. I was bewildered. Where had that question come from? My sisters had never called me black. It would have been a legitimate question, yet it hadn't come up in our home.

Racism is taught. It is the shame that accompanies it that comes unbidden, rising naturally as rain. I remember coming home from school one day in an adolescent huff. I attended John Marshall Junior High with two of my close friends, Rachel T and Rachel W. We dressed alike, acted alike and used the same slang. The three of us wore glasses and had short curly hair.

My feelings were hurt by my social studies teacher who could not keep the three of us girls straight. She looked at me with a cold flat stare and said, "I can't tell any of you apart. . . Well, it doesn't matter. . ."

I didn't hear the rest of her instruction that day. Those simple words, not as hateful as many I had heard on the playground and in the street, were uttered with such disdain, I was hurt to the core. Ms. Kempe was a teacher, a representative of the good order of things, and I respected her. If she held me in contempt, I was worth nothing. In that moment my teacher made it clear she wasn't going to learn how to tell us apart and didn't care to try. I was the slightly taller, skinny, one with thick lenses in my glasses. Rachel T was short, pretty, and had really small feet. Rachel W was the somber one, always thinking before responding. She got the high scores. How Ms. Kempe couldn't distinguish us one from another was beyond me.

I was uncharacteristically quiet that day as we walked home from school. I took care of my little sisters and slumped around the house doing my homework and chores, brooding about how my teacher had treated me. By the time my parents came home I was in a first-rate depression.

"You look like you were hit by a Mack truck. Do you feel as bad as you look?"

Jack was always joking with me, but his question sent me into a permanent pout. My mouth clamped shut and tears slid down behind my thick glasses. Jack, who had been smiling up until then, looked at me with concern. He put his arm around my shoulder.

"What's wrong?"

I slumped against him, "My teacher hates black people. She never calls on me. She doesn't even care about me." I added with fury, "I'm not doing anything for her anymore!" Then I told him with shame what had happened a school. As Jack tried to console me, I became more and more entrenched in the idea that the world wasn't fair to black people: "We never get anything!" I was intractable.

At that point he said, "You think you have a hard time? Let me tell you about the Jews." And he sat me down and recounted what happened with the Jews in Europe and why his parents fled to the United States from Ukraine.

"My parents came over just before the Russian Revolution. "They got out using their jewels for bribes. By the time they got to New York they had nothing."

I couldn't imagine how hard it must have been sneaking around, escaping the authorities. It was beyond possibility that I could go to a new country without any money, not knowing the language, and make a living. It was thrilling and scary to me all at once.

Years later, my sister Nancy found some letters

written by her grandmother, Sarah Pineles. The letters were written in an archaic form of Hebrew in a round, beautifully scripted hand. After some difficulty, Nancy, who now lives in Maryland, found someone who could translate them. One Christmas, she copied one line from a letter in calligraphy and gave it to each of us in a photo frame, together with a photograph of Grandma Sarah. The line read, "From this terrible trouble, grass will yet grow on the earth."

I am not sure why we didn't have a little pot of ethnic unrest stirring in our home. It just wasn't an issue. I was proud that I was related to a Jew, and loved my sisters' soft, blond hair. My mother was the center of our world, intelligent, steady and loving. She loved each of us individually and without reservation. We felt no need to all look alike or be cut from the same cloth. Without saying so, or maybe without being conscious of it, we were proud of our unique family in a day and age when the word, "diversity," was not used in conversations about society.

ST PAUL, MINNESOTA

LOOK HOMEWARD, ANGEL

LIFE'S PATTERNS ARE LIKE the whorls on our fingertips. They loop around and back and past each other, creating their own design in a defined space. Like the unique configuration of my fingerprints, the lines of my life's path wound extraordinarily close to those of my mother's.

When it was time to go to college, my mother wanted me to have the same rich experience she had and attend a small, liberal arts college with high standards and professors who take an interest in their students. I applied to Wellesley, Antioch and Swarthmore, and was accepted at Antioch. However, I did not get a scholarship, and my family could not afford the expense of room and board, so I settled on Macalester College and lived at home. If I had known what I do now, I would have gone to Antioch anyway, studied hard and spent the night with friends. I am sure something would have worked out for me. My mother cheered me up. She thought Macalester College would serve just as well. Her college years had been transformational, both intellectually and emotionally. It was at Macalester that she met my father, joined a commune, got political and defined herself as a woman helping to change the world.

My mother really liked one professor in particular, Dr. Ward. He was still teaching English literature when I enrolled in 1960. Dr. Ward had encouraged my mother as a gifted student and was the reason she majored in English literature. By the time I sat in his class almost 20 years later, I saw Dr. Ward as an old guy who reminded me of the distinguished movie actor, Charles Laughton. He wore a vest over his big belly, his glasses slid down his nose, and he looked over them as he lectured the class. He spoke just like Laughton, pooching his lips out as if for a kiss while his cheeks remained immobile.

My mother hoped that once in college, I would mature a bit and give up my teenage behavior— fast-talking, eyes catching others' to share a joke, and looking for an opportunity to make people laugh. Dr. Ward could not have been impressed with the sassy black girl who sat before him in class. Years later I found a paper I had written in my mother's basement critiquing Yeats' poem, *Leda and the Swan*. At the time, I am not sure I even understood what the rape meant, much less the symbolism in the events which followed, but I wrote a long interpretation of the sonnet. It was embarrassing to reread.

I am sure I was not the only student in Dr. Ward's class more interested in socializing than in literature, so it was not surprising that he seized our attention at the outset with a rigorous assignment: Write a term paper proving that when Shakespeare wrote his sonnets, he had read Ovid's *Metamorphoses*. I didn't know what a sonnet was, and I had never heard of Ovid. Now, I would have to master both so that I could detect identical phraseology in them. This was before the days of computer searches, which could have really helped me do the assignment. I poured over the texts and cried and protested to my mother. She tried to help, but when it comes down to it, there is no substitute for studying, thinking, and understanding. I had to get down to work. My typed paper was twenty pages long. Although I'm sure I found some common words and phrases, I am not sure that I demonstrated any real comprehension of what either Ovid or Shakespeare wrote. We were also required to memorize the sonnet, "Let me not to the marriage of true minds admit impediments," along with the Prologue to the *Canterbury Tales*. I can recite them both today.

Another challenging professor was Wild Bill Hickock, a stern, desiccated curlicue of a man, about five feet tall, with the reputation of a tyrant. My humanities class was small, a half dozen of us, and I was excited to take it. I loved literature and philosophy, and considered majoring in humanities, a perfect combination of the two. Dr. Hickock's required reading list for the semester was extensive. There were eighteen titles: *Paradise Lost, Paradise Regained, War and Peace, The Red and the Black,* James Joyce's *Ulysses, The Great Gatsby,* and a number of other classics. Dr. Hickock's lectures did not help me understand the books, nor how they were related to each other. I took notes in class, scribbling down everything Dr. Hickock said as fast as I could, but I was lost in the sea of words.

When we sat for our final exam, we were given a blue book and a half sheet of paper with five questions typed on it. They were short and asked about arcane details of only two or three of the many titles. I remember the answer to one was in a footnote. The questions did not go to the major themes, which was what I had studied. I was lucky to have finished the reading list and had no idea what the answers to Dr. Hickock's questions were.

With my blue book open to two blank pages before me, I sat in my seat thinking. Finally, I picked up my pen and wrote, "I don't know the answers to these questions, but here are some I can answer." I made up questions, wrote them down and answered them. I filled the pages of the blue book with what was going on in *Paradise Lost* and the plot of *War and Peace*, and managed to work in most of the information I had memorized for the final exam.

Two weeks later semester grades came in the mail. I was aghast. Dr. Hickock gave me an F. In high school I had never received a grade lower than the C I received in physics. The failing grade literally took the breath out of me. When I took the exam I was sure Dr. Hickock would appreciate that even though I didn't know the answers, I had tried, and I demonstrated that I had read and studied the material.

My mother told me to make an appointment to see Dr. Hickock. When I did, it was clear that my attempt to pass the exam was not well received. He was insulted by my improvisation. I entreated with him to change the grade. I could not take home an F in his class. Finally, he relented.

"I will tell you what," he said. "If you memorize Milton's poem, *Lycidas,* recite it line for line without so much as a single error, I will reconsider giving you a passing grade." I bobbed my head in agreement, relieved to get a chance to redeem myself. Dr. Hickock pulled out a copy of the poem and handed it to me. It was three single-spaced pages long. I gulped and left his office.

"How can I possibly memorize three pages?" I wailed to my mother when I got home. She soothed me and reassured that it wasn't too hard. She showed me how the poem was written in iambic pentameter and helped me memorize each line. She explained that the poem was about the accidental death at sea of Milton's close friend. After much practice, I could finally recite all three pages of the famous elegy perfectly. I made an appointment with Dr. Hickock.

"Are you ready?" I was standing in front of him in his little office.

I nodded my head.

"Remember, if you make even one mistake, or miss a single word, I will fail you instantly."

"I know," I responded, and I began.

When I finished, Dr. Hickock sat there with no expression on his face. I didn't know if I had made a mistake or not. He just stared at me, looking like a dried up insect in his leather armchair. Finally, he exhaled and said, "That was correct."

The recitation had gone off without a hitch! I went home high as a kite. I knew I wouldn't get an A in the course because the professor did not like what I thought was a can-do attitude, but I hoped for a B. In a few weeks my revised grade came in the mail. There it was, Humanities 101, Grade— D. True to his word Wild Bill Hickock had given me a passing grade. I was so ashamed and intimidated by the course load, I did not have the heart to fight it.

At the same time, I was having other troubles at Macalester. At first, things were going all right. I got contact lenses when I was eighteen, and whether they bothered me or not, I had no idea. I was so invested in putting away my thick, coke-bottle glasses that I took to the lenses instantly. Getting rid of my glasses changed my self-image and gave me confidence. I felt like a normal person and felt I could be pretty.

Going to Macalester was like attending a much smaller high school on a much bigger campus. Central High, where I had graduated, had 2,000 students. Macalester's total enrollment was 600, and like Central High, they were all young. I had always been outgoing and quickly made friends. We often met at the Old Main and then strolled across campus to our classes laughing and talking.

In my sophomore year Jack decided he wanted to teach high school. By then he had earned a masters in chemistry and, except for a couple of required classes, had all the coursework needed for a teacher's credential. To save money, we both signed up for human physiology and shared the textbook, which cost sixty-seven dollars. Jack didn't need the book because he knew the material already. In fact, all semester, he corrected the professor about inaccuracies in his presentation. It must have been annoying. It was certainly embarrassing to me. Finally, when we got to the study of blood and the circulatory system, the professor turned the class over to Jack and asked him to teach the unit. Jack had done blood work in hospital labs for years. The material was second nature to him.

I was mortified to see Jack lecturing in front of the class. He no longer presented the handsome, cocky figure that I admired when I was nine years old. He wore a long unbuttoned tweed overcoat whose front went flapping open when he walked to reveal a plaid lumberjack shirt and grey twill Sears trousers. He wore high-top fur-lined men's slippers because they were cheaper than winter boots. These were in fact the same slippers he was wearing when he ran out of gas on that fateful drive to Stillwater and had to hike a few miles in the snow before someone picked him up. Jack struck me as a modern-day Mr. Macawber, someone my friends and I would have made malicious fun of if he weren't my stepfather.

Most days my friends and I lined up in the cafeteria to buy a drink, get a table and eat our bag lunches together. Jack loved tushes, and when he passed me on line, he would walk right by without saying a word and pinch my bottom. I was used to it and routinely swatted his hand away without a break in my sentence, but other people in the cafeteria who saw it raised their eyebrows and probably wondered about this dirty old man.

By the end of my sophomore year there were other problems. At heart I was still a city girl and no longer enjoyed Macalester's bucolic campus. Most of the students were from wealthy families. I did not fit in. They dressed in fashionable pleated skirts and cashmere sweaters and wore makeup. Many had their own cars. I wore homemade clothes and sweaters, which, though beautiful, did not compare to the expensive finery of my classmates. Moreover, the students were mostly white. Most of the few black students were from Africa, including Kofi Annan, who went on to become the Secretary General of the United Nations. My upbringing in New York City made me hunger for a campus with an urban feel and people of all ages and races. I had gone folk dancing at the University of Minnesota since I was fifteen, so I was familiar with the milieu of a diverse campus, as opposed to that of this parochial, Presbyterian endowed college.

"I want to go to a proletarian school and be with all kinds of people," I pleaded with my mother. Still driven by the need to identify and belong, I said, "I would be embarrassed to say I graduated from Macalester."

After much discussion, I went to the University of Minnesota for my last two years of college. I loved its enormous campus, its granite buildings, and the wide variety of people from all walks of life. I graduated with a double major in math and philosophy and minors in French and political science. At sea at Macalester, I felt I might drown there. I had unwittingly followed Milton's advice in Lycidas and looked landward, to the urban campus of the University of Minnesota. It was like going home.

Look homeward Angel now, and melt with ruth;
And, O ye dolphins, waft the hapless youth.

~John Milton, *Lycidas*

ST PAUL, MINNESOTA

THE FIRST TIME

THE FIRST TIME I MADE LOVE I got pregnant, an accident that triggered an incredible stream of events that eventually landed me in California and is the reason why I live here today over 50 years later. My girlfriend and I had gotten permission to hang out at a friend's house, but we actually went to the home of her boyfriend. It was Sunday night of President's Day, a three-day weekend at the University of Minnesota where I was a junior. I was nineteen years old.

Ron's mother was out, so we had the house to ourselves. The house was dark, the only light coming from the foyer and the hall next to the living room. A stack of rhythm and blues 45-records was playing on the record player with the fat plastic insert that accommodated their larger center. James Brown's impassioned, *Please, Please Please*, should have been my clue, but I was so green that when Gladys and Ron went off to a nearby room, I didn't catch on to where the evening was headed.

> *My love must be a kind of blind love*
> *I can't see anyone but you*
>   ~ The Flamingos, *I Only Have Eyes For You* [11]

---

[11] Warren, Harry and Harry Dubin. I Only Have Eyes For You. The Flamingoes, 1959.

My boyfriend, James and I were fooling around on the couch. We had necked many times before, but never without the usual roadblocks provided by parent supervision. We had never gone, "all the way." He was a dreamy-looking guy, tall, with fair, pecan colored skin and large, wide-spaced eyes and long eyelashes. Ron said James and I were fated for each other because we were both mixed-race kids in odd family situations. James was one of several kids in a foster home run by a pious woman. James had a beautiful voice and he sang late into the night with his friends in front of the liquor store on the corner of Rondo and Dale, head cocked sideways, snapping his fingers and leaning in to croon. He would thrust his hands in his pockets and pull up his pants to reveal long, black-stockinged ankles. It was the doo-wap time of soul music, and could he sing! James and I were fated for each other, all right, but not in a good way.

I heard a moan in the other room from Gladys, and then a stifled giggle. I had never heard the sounds of love-making before, but James knew what it meant, and, realizing the coast was clear, started making love to me in earnest.

It was over in minutes. I was surprised. It was so mechanical. I hadn't experienced the expected powerful onrush of passion I had expected.

Later on, I did feel something, though. I missed

my period. Not sure I that I was really pregnant, I waited another month. Still no period.

I said nothing to anyone, not even Gladys. This couldn't be. I could NOT get pregnant. By the time May came, I was worried. My predicament was clearly not resolving itself. This may have been the first adult responsibility I was to face in my life.

I turned to a mutual friend of a few of us high school kids. Her name was Sharon Lee Ward. Sharon was a black woman, an anthropology PhD candidate at the University of Minnesota and lived in South Minneapolis. She was a real interesting lady, about 28 years of age, although we thought of her as much older, bright, articulate and political. We all revered her. She lived with her boyfriend, who sold marijuana, and regaled us with her stories and exploits. Sharon had come up from the South in the '50s as part of the great Negro migration. She arrived in Chicago alone, with no skills, and no family, seeking a better life and made a living as a prostitute. Somehow she got a law degree from John Marshall, a prestigious law school in Chicago, and was now a graduate student the U of M. Her thesis was about the social implications of prostitution. I loved Sharon because she was fearless and didn't care who heard her speaking the truth.

I confided my problem to Sharon, who said with a chuckle, "Hell, I can take care of that for you."

"You can get me an abortion?" My eyes teared up with hope. My back was up against a wall. I had asked my stepfather, Jack, who was a chemist in a hospital lab to give me something to abort, but he was too principled to be any part of it. Though he was sympathetic and nonjudgmental, he refused to get me pills that would cause me to miscarry.

"I can't do that. It is illegal, and I could lose my job." Jack was always ethical. He wasn't afraid of dealing with the truth, and he refused to lie.

I finally broke down and told my mother that I was pregnant and somehow had to get an abortion. She grew upset and begged me not to do go through with it.

"Please, I'll raise the baby if only you will deliver it," she implored.

My mother's response took me by surprise, but didn't move me. I think it might have made a difference if she had told me that she was speaking from experience. She had gotten pregnant when she fell in love with my father. This was before I was born. She got an abortion, but I didn't learn that until decades later. I might have understood the passion with which she warned me, but I was young, tunnel-visioned, and unable to hear the genuine sorrow in my mother's pleas. I was in a bind. I was a "good girl." No one must know that I had had sex, much less that I had gotten pregnant.

My mother was adamant. She tried one more time.

"Don't make a decision that you will regret for the rest of your life."

She insisted that I see a psychiatrist, hoping he would change my mind, and made an appointment for me at the University. But the counseling session was a sterile interchange, the psychiatrist risking nothing to make a personal connection, and I, already guarded, not giving anything. I was getting an abortion, and that was it.

*   *   *

"Sure. I can do it myself," Sharon said. "It's not complicated. People been doing it for generations."

Abortion was illegal at the time, and there was no safe way to end a pregnancy. I didn't care. I had to get back to normal. Looking back at this horrendous train of events, I am astonished because my problem needn't have been fraught with secrecy and risk. I cannot forgive myself.

First, Sharon told me to drink a bottle of castor oil. She said it would bring on stomach cramps and trigger a miscarriage. The stuff tasted so bad that I froze it in a cocktail ice cube tray and drank the cubes down with orange juice. I got sick to my stomach all right, but no miscarriage. Then Sharon said that for $200 she would give me some pills that would take care of the problem. I emptied my long unused savings account and gave her the money. That didn't work, either. I was too far along. By this time, it was June, and I was desperate.

My friend, Gladys had spent the night with me and we were in my room getting dressed the next morning. She turned to me. "You're gaining weight," she commented, looking at my midsection. I didn't catch the hint, and didn't learn until later that she and I shared the same problem. We had both gotten pregnant the same night. I hadn't noticed that she had a little belly, but she had noticed mine. We were all of 115 pounds at the time.

It was time for the abortion. One evening Sharon had me come over to her house. I lay on my back on her kitchen table, and she gave me a coat-hanger abortion. It was as simple as straightening a steel coat hanger and using it to puncture the placenta inside my uterus. A couple of days later I woke up in a lake of blood in my bed. The blood scared me, and I called to my mother, not realizing I was hemorrhaging. I thought I had started my period but that something more must be wrong. My mother was lightning quick at putting two and two together, and rushed me to the University of Minnesota Hospital, where I had student health coverage.

By then I was well into my fourth month of pregnancy and experiencing real labor pains. At one point I left the emergency room waiting area to go to the bathroom. When I looked in the toilet, I saw the fetus, no bigger than my finger. I was horrified and shocked. It had fingernails. What had I done?

In short order, I was in a hospital bed staring up into the faces of an administrator, a doctor and nurses on both sides of me.

"Who did this to you?"

I didn't answer. Wouldn't say.

"We want to help you, but you have to tell us first: Who gave you this abortion?"

They insisted, but instinctively, I wanted to protect Sharon from trouble that I had caused. I didn't care if I died. Delirious with pain, I simply didn't respond. Finally, I was taken to surgery where a D&C procedure was performed, dilation and curettage. My uterus was scraped out and emptied. I was given blood transfusions and stayed the night.

*   *   *

When I got home I found my eyes welling up, and tears were running down my cheeks. A huge sadness overtook me. My mother tried to get me to talk about it.

"What's wrong?" she coaxed.

"Why are you crying?"

I didn't know. I was too immature to process that I was grieving over the loss of a life within me.

"I don't know," I replied. "I just feel sad." I wept silently, without words. Tears leaked down my face without warning throughout the day.

Again, my mother took me to the psychiatrist who diagnosed me with postpartum depression. I didn't take any medication. He said it was normal in cases where the pregnancy was as far advanced as mine, and would probably go away in a few days. The depression stayed with me for the entire summer and certainly colored the rest of my life. I don't know how I got through final exams that spring.

In June, Gladys and Ron got married in a shotgun wedding. I was one of her bridesmaids and wore a canary yellow satin fishtail dress, à la Diana Ross and the Supremes. To my great embarrassment, milk leaked from my breasts and stained the bodice.

I got pregnant again almost right away and managed to miscarry with the pills Sharon had originally given me. My mother then got me birth control pills, but forgot to tell me it takes a full month before they kick in. I got pregnant a third time, and aborted again. By this time I was an emotional mess.

Now, it was September. The Vietnam War was going strong, and James was called up for the draft. He came to me and said, "If you marry me, I won't have to join the Army."

What could I do? I was racked with guilt. What

kind of woman aborts her child and refuses to marry the man who made her pregnant? I accepted James's proposal, and we planned a wedding at the home of one of my girlfriends on September 24. I sewed my wedding dress and my mother made lasagna and a wedding cake.

Both Jack and my mother had tried to talk me out of getting married. "You don't know what you are getting into. You are just kids. You are not prepared for the responsibility of marriage."

But I had lost my own agency. I no longer saw myself as worthy of making decisions in my own self-interest. I was resigned to a life in the black community, Scotch-taping spit curls to the side of my cheeks, drinking whisky sours, and playing whist. When my mother reminded me that I wanted to go to Europe, travel, and get a graduate degree, it seemed she was talking about a stranger. My life was over. I had thrown it away, along with the lives of three babies.

James and I got an apartment in Minneapolis and split the rent with another couple. They, like me, were students at the University. It was my senior year, and I graduated from the University of Minnesota in March. James got a job as a trainee at a Bank of America, and I got a job as a research analyst with the State of Minnesota writing statistical reports describing the activities of the various kinds of mental facilities run by the state.

Within months, James was fired. It seemed he had been absent too many times. His excuses grew in magnitude, from being sick to illness in the family. Finally, he told the bank that the reason he was absent was because his mother had died. They sent flowers to her house for her funeral. Their arrival at her door made her indignant. She refused them and called the bank to complain. James was immediately fired.

In the meantime, he had bought a rifle and a brand new cobalt-blue Ford Mustang. He had no way to cover the payments. I was saddled with our share of the rent as well as his bills. One night we were lying on our backs in bed, bickering about money.

"Shut up!" he said.

But I was used to yakking my head off and had not picked up on the warning signs of a man under growing pressure from his family, his friends, and now his wife. I kept yammering on.

Bam! James grabbed me by my shoulders, threw me up against the wall and punched me. The bedroom was totally dark, yet I saw everything I needed to. I slid down the wall, sitting back on my heels for a few minutes, and then quietly lay down in bed next to him without a word.

The next morning, I called my mother in Beloit, Wisconsin. She told me to get on a bus immediately and come home. Numb, I complied. I was too overwhelmed with the disaster of the marriage I had entered in to be ashamed. I told my mother the entire story. She lent me the family VW Microbus, and I drove back to St. Paul, some 300 miles, loaded it up with everything I owned and drove back to Beloit, all in one day.

My mother now had her opening. She talked to me again about graduate school, and I applied to the University of Wisconsin and was accepted in a program to earn a masters in social work. Class did not start for three weeks. Fearful that I might reconcile with James, my mother suggested that I go out to California and visit our longtime family friends, Sally and John Rue. This was the same John who had taken care of me when my mother and I first arrived in New York City. John was a professor of political science at Stanford, and he lived with his wife and two children in Menlo Park. I took a Greyhound bus out to the West Coast.

While I stayed with John and Sally, they loaned me their two-toned, turquoise and white, Buick LeSabre, and I drove up to the University of California to go folk dancing. I had been a regular folk dancer at the University of Minnesota, and loved the Greek and Baltic dances best. The place was full of hippies, many of them high on LSD.

The Free Speech Movement and the Summer of Love were coming, and the color of the air was lavender. I couldn't resist it. I called my mother and told her I wasn't coming home. I would go to graduate school at UC Berkeley.

That is how I came to live in California.

EPILOGUE

OVERCOMING ADVERSITY

BECAUSE OF A belligerent, rebellious attitude, I was expelled or politely asked to leave every elementary school I attended. I think my mother's pacific shyness was part of the reason I early developed a robust sense of justice and fought with anyone I felt was in the wrong. Another reason for my militancy resides in the conditions of my early years, which forced me to be independent and resourceful. What started as a rough, tumultuous childhood ended with gaining a family, security, and a good education, notwithstanding my teenage pregnancies and disastrous first marriage. These events left me off kilter emotionally and help to explain the choices I was to make when I came to live in California.

However, the turbulence in my life had started generations before in the lives of both my parents. My mother was born in 1918, in St. Paul. Her mother died when she was five years old, essentially leaving her and her younger sister orphans to be farmed among family relatives until her paternal grandmother took them in. Her father was an alcoholic, and their home life was unstable because he spent most of his paycheck on alcohol. My mother's family were no-nonsense Norwegian immigrants who had landed in Stevens Point, Wisconsin during the Civil War and settled throughout Wisconsin, Minnesota,

South Dakota, and on into Montana and California. They were not prepared for the cultural shift that each new generation brings.

My father's birth in 1910 to a poor family in a rural area outside Wilkes Barre, Pennsylvania was unremarked, and his home life short-lived. By the time he was twelve he was living by his wits on the street. When I read Richard Wright's, *Native Son* in high school, I was struck by how similar his life was to Bigger Thomas's, and began to understand that the conditions of his childhood were not unusual for many black people. While my mother was a blond, blue-eyed apple-cheeked beauty, my father was a black man, hard-edged and suave, forced to survive on his own. They were bound to be attracted to one another.

My mother and father came to Macalester College on similar paths, both the first in their families to attend college and neither having the family support to pay for expenses. They worked their way through college and earned degrees in English literature. My mother worked full-time in a canning factory. Each was propelled to escape the Depression, my mother unaware she was headed for the middle class, and my father equally unaware he would become a totem for the typical black male, unemployed and poor, with unfulfilled dreams.

My mother and father fell in love before racially-mixed marriages were acceptable. It wasn't until 1967, thirty years after they met, that the Supreme Court ruled interracial marriages legal. Tragically, their marriage did not work.

When my mother grabbed me and fled to New York City, for her, it was an escape, exciting, and at the same time, fraught with danger, which made it even more of an adventure— for both of us. In my mother's autobiography, she wrote:

> *There has always been something in me that takes delight in impossible situations, as though I face a dilemma with the thought, "Well, here is a quandary. How am I going to get out of it?" There is the excitement, the challenge, of a sort of epic experience.*
> ~ Lila Rogers Pineles, 1994

Even though I was a baby at the time, I think that in nonverbal ways I understood what was happening, however, I did not come to fully appreciate it until I was an adult. My mother and I were poor in things that can be bought with money, and had many exciting adventures because of that, but we were rich in experiences that money cannot buy.

My early years were spent shifting between Minnesota and New York. Every move was a response to a problem. The schools I attended reflected the various cultural backgrounds I was exposed to in New York and the

Twin Cities. The private school on Park Avenue was white, upper class, Protestant, and elite. P.S. 33 on Manhattan's West Side was a much tougher school where my classmates were Spanish speakers whose fathers worked on the docks. In Minnesota, I attended a black parochial school, and my teachers were nuns. We went through the stations of the cross as part of the school day, and I loved the Roman Catholic church service, which was so similar to the Episcopal church we had attended in New York. Back in the Bronx, I was the only black kid at P.S. 95, which served a Jewish community in the Bronx. Later, I again attended various rural and urban schools in the Twin Cities.

However, by the time our family bought a house and settled down in the black community of St. Paul, things were not completely normal. My mother, Jack, and my two sisters were white, and blond with blue eyes. They were all shorter than I, who was kind of the giant sequoia in the family picture. We loved each other unconditionally and had a dog and a piano, everything I had dreamed of since I was little. Yet, as a teenager, I knew my family picture did not mirror that of my African-American friends.

Civil rights sit-in demonstration against racial discrimination. Woolworth's Dimestore, Minneapolis, 1960. Courtesy St. Paul Dispatch and Pioneer Press

NAACP picketing at a shopping mall.
That's my friend in the middle. See how her scarf is knotted on her chin? We girls used to do that because we thought it made us look tough. Father Denzel Carty, the priest at my Episcopal Church was one of the organizers. Senator Hubert Humphrey came out and supported us.

~ Courtesy St. Paul Dispatch and Pioneer Press

My mother attended Socialist Workers Party meetings and hosted League of Women's Voters luncheons. She sent me door to door to collect donations for the Women's International League for Peace and Freedom, and instead of a swank Ford Fairlane or a Cadillac, status symbols in the community, parked at the curb, all five of us fit into a light blue VW bug, the only car of its kind in the community. My mother volunteered me to sit in support of the Freedom Bus Rides at the Woolworth's counter in Minneapolis. She was too shy to do it herself, and I was too dumb and naïve to appreciate why it was important.

My mother and my sisters and I went to a neighborhood Episcopal Church, while my friends attended Baptist and AME Methodist churches. My stepfather, Jack was an ardent Zionist, and had declared himself an atheist. He delivered diatribes against organized religion at our Sunday dinners after church. He would sit at one end of the dining room table and my mother at the other with us kids on both sides in between.

At these Sunday afternoon dinners my parents discussed politics and literature. Jack explained why Roosevelt was America's greatest president and Beethoven was the finest classical composer. Our house was filled with books, and in summer, the sounds of classical music could be heard on the sidewalk through the drapes at the windows. When I was bored, I would select one of the books and read. There were no games to distract me on an android phone or video game player.

I had a formula for a happy life: Get a family— a mother, a father, siblings, a dog and a piano. My deep need to be rooted, to be secure, drove me to seek these key elements of happiness. By the time I was eleven, our family— black, white, Jewish and Christian, all rolled into one— had moved into our own home in the black neighborhood of St. Paul. It was concentric circles: black kid, white family, in a black community, in the predominantly white state of Minnesota. My mother was a Norwegian Christian, my stepfather a Russian Jew, and I was plaid.

My upbringing was rich and culturally diverse and my family was multi-ethnic before the concept was popularized. Because we were poor, we moved a lot. We lived in urban, ghetto, rural, and suburban communities. I lived and played with children in white, Jamaican, Italian, Puerto Rican, Jewish, and black neighborhoods, and I have attended public, private, rural and parochial elementary schools. I consider myself fortunate to have grown up in such a richly diverse set of circumstances.

*   *   *

Years and years later, after I married a black man, a Jew, and a white man for good measure, and after I raised an interracial family of my own in a house with a piano and a succession of dogs, I realize that I have fulfilled my blueprint for happiness. My life's path was remarkably similar to that of my mother. I was also a member of an alternative community, Synanon Foundation, Inc., that was committed to reforming society. I reflect on my life today and think that it is only natural to strive to be happy. It is as natural as it is for plants to grow toward the sun. That need is what drove me during my childhood.

In Synanon my friends and I talked about the importance of enthusiasm. Self-help gurus today say attitude is everything, and they are right. The word enthusiasm comes from the Greek, *entheos*, which means, *the god within*. I think from the time I was very little, my enthusiasm carried me through hard times, turning them into adventures. It also helped me solve problems. I succeeded in getting an education and securing the ability to exercise options. I realize I am lucky. My mother provided us a full family and is the reason for my success, and it all started when she literally saved my life by running away to New York City.

April 2017

ABOUT THE AUTHOR

After Sandra Rogers-Hare retired from a career in education she has been writing books. She presently facilitates a writers workshop at the San Leandro Public Library. She also conducts English proficiency testing for public school students and is interested in aspects of second-language learning. She travels, studies history and takes photographs. The second book of her memoir, *Salmagundi, Living in Utopia*, will be published in 2018. Sandra lives in San Leandro, California

Salmagundi *~ Living in Utopia*

Sandra's next book picks up her story from her arrival in California and recounts her life in the San Francisco Bay Area, graduate school at UC Berkeley, her entry into the teaching profession in Berkeley, and her experience living and working in a controversial utopian community called Synanon. To be published in 2018.